ESSENTIAL
SEA
KAYAKING

OTHER BOOKS BY THE AUTHOR

The Ragged Mountain Press Guide to Outdoor Sports—Skills and Knowledge for the Whole Outdoors (with Roseann Hanson)

Complete Sea Kayak Touring

Southern Arizona Nature Almanac (with Roseann Hanson)

50 Common Reptiles and Amphibians of the Southwest

ESSENTIAL
SEA
KAYAKING

JONATHAN HANSON

The Lyons Press

Printed in Canada

First edition

Designed by PageMasters & Company

10   9   8   7   6   5   4   3   2   1

Library of Congress Cataloging-in-Publication Data
Hanson, Jonathan
    Essential sea kayaking / by Jonathan Hanson.
      p. cm.
    Includes index.
    ISBN 1-55821-715-0 (pbk.)
    1. Sea kayaking. I. Title.
GV788.5.H364   2000
797.1'224—dc21   99-29092
                                                 CIP

CONTENTS

Contents

ACKNOWLEDGMENTS

Every book represents the efforts and knowledge of not just its author but of many individuals—friends, family, colleagues, and even strangers who added immeasurably to the quality of the project. It is impossible to name them all, but I would like to try. Of course, any errata in text, photos, or captions are strictly mine.

Many thanks to the staff at *Sea Kayaker* magazine for their years of confidence and friendship: Chris Cunningham, former editor Karen Matthee, and Leslie Forsberg.

To the staff at *Outside* magazine and *Outside Magazine Buyer's Guide* I also owe a great debt, particularly to Eric Hagerman and Bob Howells, whose help and confidence are always above and beyond.

I also want to thank Jeff Serena, formerly of Ragged Mountain Press, whose recommendations helped get me going on several book projects.

Of many equipment manufacturers who helped me over the years, Tom and Lisa Derrer of Eddyline Kayaks were especially supportive and helpful.

And to my many paddling partners I want to give particularly heartfelt thanks for companionship, education, and, of course, good fodder for writing: Michael Cox, Tommy Thompson, John Gentile and Katie Iverson, and Roseann, who is my life companion as well.

INTRODUCTION
A WORLD OF ADVENTURE

I'm going to make a blanket statement: No other outdoor sport in the world is as easy to get started in as sea kayaking, yet no other outdoor sport in the world offers such an astonishing scope for real adventure.

Here's my evidence, in 200 words or less:

Even if you've never been in a boat you can climb into a sea kayak and, with no instruction whatsoever, make decent progress across a sheltered harbor or bay. To move forward you pull the double-bladed paddle through the water first on one side, then the other. To turn left (assuming your kayak has a foot-controlled rudder, as most do), you push with your left foot; to go right, you push with your right foot. To stop, paddle backward. That's it.

Yet with experience and practice, you can in that same kayak undertake self-contained expeditions to some of the most remote regions of our planet: the Arctic coast of Canada, the fjords of Chile and Argentina, the islands of the Sea of Cortez. You can carry inside the kayak everything you need to live comfortably for weeks at a time, completely independent of civilization.

See what I mean?

Okay—obviously, there are some nuances to master in terms of paddling proficiency, and the jump from "never been in a boat" to "with experience and practice" covers a lot of ground. But my point, of course, is that the basics of sea kayaking do not require weeks of preparation and training. Nor do you have to spend two months circumnavigating Madagascar for the sport to be enjoyable. One of my favorite pastimes is puttering around harbors looking at sailboats. I also love bird-watching from a kayak, or just paddling offshore a mile or so to experience sunset alone over a calm, empty sea. I have friends who *commute* in their kayaks in seaport towns, and other friends, biologists, who use them for research. One woman I know is content to paddle around the pond near her home and listen to loons calling in the morning—

wonderful. It's not just the depth, but the breadth of experience it offers that makes the sea kayak such a wonderful craft. The icing on the cake is that you're in a vehicle that not only produces no pollution or noise, but keeps you in great shape as well.

With all that said, I must add this: Anyone who takes up sea kayaking should make a commitment to being a serious student. Far too many paddlers sign up for a guided trip or two, or spend a half-dozen afternoons practicing on a lake, then assume they have the sport mastered and head for Alaska. Wrong. Oh, to be sure, thousands of such people accomplish major trips with no trouble, but when the unexpected happens they're helpless. In these cases the ease with which a beginning sea kayaker can master basic strokes and turns is misleading, for the ocean is a complex entity with many moods—not all of them benign. Serious paddlers learn in advance to handle all the conditions with which they might be faced—and are prepared when and if those conditions hit.

The best way to become a truly proficient sea kayaker is through a combination of reading, practice, and professional instruction. Reading a book such as this one provides a firm grounding in equipment, terminology, theory, and technique. Practice helps ingrain basic techniques to the point of instinct. And professional instruction is invaluable for speeding up the process, since an experienced observer can point out flaws in technique that might take weeks or months for the self-taught to uncover. I urge you to combine this book with as many classes as you can; your self-confidence will peak rapidly.

I'm often asked to recommend exercises for sea kayaking. My answer is always the same: Get out and paddle! There aren't any special muscle groups you need to precondition for paddling, as long as you don't push too hard at first. If you tend toward back problems, pay close attention to how you feel while paddling, and make sure your seat is comfortable and supportive.

You'll notice that throughout this book I'll hammer hard on safety issues such as life jackets, proper clothing, emergency signaling equipment, and rescue techniques. That's not because sea kayaking is dangerous; in fact, it's because sea kayaking is an extremely safe sport, and I'd like to keep it that way. The very few tragedies that occur each year almost invariably involve an inexcusable lack of proper equipment or ignorance of technique. To me, having the right knowledge and equipment, and being prepared to handle any situation that might arise, is part of the adventure.

The final, but most important, part of becoming a sea kayaker is developing a sense of stewardship for the landscape through which you travel. Just as it's easier to appreciate your surroundings while paddling quietly along a virgin coast, so do clear-cuts and garbage and oil spills take on a more immediate horror.

The vast majority of people who never contact their legislators avoid it not because they're lazy, but because they think one voice won't make a difference, especially in the face of massive lobbying by the extractive industries that make fortunes from public lands. Those people are wrong, for both representatives and senators (whose primary drive, let's face it, is to get reelected by people like you) state time and time again that every phone call or e-mail message they receive makes an enormous impact, precisely *because* so few people bother. Your voice does make a difference, and with e-mail and cell phones at our beckoning there's certainly no other excuse. So please help preserve the last wild areas with which our world is blessed. Happy paddling.

PART ONE

THE EQUIPMENT

You could easily start sea kayaking with just four pieces of equipment: a boat, a paddle, a spray skirt, and a life jacket.

Of course, there are many more items you can add, and some you definitely should. But I want to give you an idea of the essential simplicity of the sport. Another great thing about sea-kayaking equipment is that, so far at least, the industry has seen very little of the "make it cheaper, not better" disease that afflicts almost every other area of consumer goods. The companies that make kayaking equipment are generally small by corporation standards, and still take great pride in their products. If you buy a good name-brand kayak, paddle, spray skirt, or other accessory, you are almost assured of many years of fine service.

CHAPTER 1

THE KAYAK

In addition to representing your largest cash outlay, the kayak will be your most bewildering purchase. Even the smallest shops now stock many models, and the total available number reaches into the hundreds. To further complicate matters, you will be bombarded by as many different opinions as there are salespeople as to which is the best material, brand, length, width, style, configuration, and color.

The best way to simplify your choice is to break it down into components. Decide first which style of kayak will suit you: single or double, traditional or sit-on-top, rigid-hull or folding. Then decide on materials: plastic, fiberglass, and so forth. Finally, you can actually try some boats to see which particular model fits you best and feels most comfortable.

SIT-ON-TOP KAYAKS

The traditional sea kayak—the direct descendant of Inuit hunting craft from the Arctic—has a fairly deep hull, and a deck that encloses a more or less oval cockpit opening. You sit inside the

3

boat, actually slightly below the waterline, and a spray skirt made of nylon or neoprene fits around the cockpit rim and your torso, preventing paddle drips and waves from getting water inside.

Recently a different style of boat (which some purists are reluctant to even call a "kayak") has been gaining popularity, especially among beginners and casual paddlers. Called a sit-on-top or wash-deck kayak, this design has no enclosed cockpit; you sit in a molded depression right out in the open. There's no spray skirt.

There are several advantages to sit-on-top kayaks. First, and most important, the boats are designed so that no self-rescue skills, such as Eskimo rolling, are needed. If the boat capsizes, you simply climb back on as if to a surfboard or sailboard (or inflatable pool toy, as the purists would archly point out). Most sit-on-top kayaks are fairly wide, and thus very stable in smooth or moderately choppy water, rendering the chance of capsize low in the first place. They're great for swimming, snorkeling, even scuba diving, since you can jump on and off at will. Some models have a built-in recess for strapping down a scuba tank.

But sit-on-tops have their downsides as well. The cockpit recess in which you sit is usually self-bailing—most of the water that gets in automatically drains back out. Nevertheless, you are always exposed to this water, and are always wet to some degree. Since you are also exposed to the wind, you must dress carefully to avoid hypothermia in any but the most tropical waters.

When those waters get rough the sit-on-top can be harder to control than a traditional design, because it's impossible to lock yourself to the boat with your knees, as you can in an enclosed cockpit. Most sit-on-tops have foot straps, which help; some have thigh straps, which help even more. But you still won't feel the same welded-in sensation you get with a properly fitting enclosed cockpit.

Although sit-on-tops offer storage compartments, their cargo capacity is significantly less than what's available in an equivalent traditional design. This, coupled with the exposed paddling position, leaves the sit-on-top with an almost insurmountable disadvantage for long-distance touring, particularly in northern latitudes.

I started out with a decided prejudice against sit-on-top kayaks. To me they lacked the grace inherent in traditional designs, and I was even a bit resentful that a novice could just hop on and paddle, with none of the investment in technique required to master a traditional kayak. I *still* think most sit-on-tops are pretty ugly, but my remaining prejudices have largely diminished. The user-friendliness of sit-on-top kayaks really is wonderful for introducing new paddlers to the joys of self-propelled boating. My current view is this: If your kayaking plans involve nothing more than day trips in temperate waters or (at most) an occasional, lightly loaded overnight or weekend excursion; if you want to use your boat for snorkeling or scuba diving: if you're hesitant or fearful to learn and practice the rescue strategies necessary to master a traditional kayak, then by all means consider a sit-on-top.

ENCLOSED-COCKPIT SEA KAYAKS

While sit-on-top kayaks have their places, the most complete range of capabilities in the world of sea kayaks still lies with the traditional designs. Sitting in the cockpit of a traditional kayak, with a spray skirt sealing off the lower part of your body, you are well protected from cold seas and wind (in warm weather, you can paddle without the skirt if you like). When the waves start to kick up, you can brace your knees under the deck, locking you and the boat

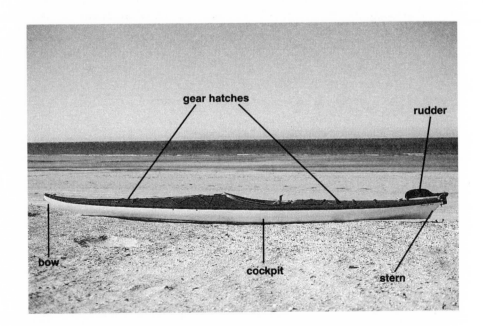

together and enabling you to maintain control even in very rough conditions. The sealed cargo compartments in the front and rear of the boat hold a tremendous amount of gear, making voyages of a week or 10 days a piece of cake and allowing, with careful packing, self-contained expeditions of a month or more. Those compartments also act as built-in air chambers, providing safe buoyancy even if the boat is heavily loaded and the cockpit is filled with water. The seats in traditional boats usually offer much more back support than the rudimentary depressions in sit-on-tops, making long paddling days more comfortable.

Newcomers to sea kayaking worry about capsizing. It is certainly possible to capsize a sea kayak, but keep in mind several things. First, the broad *beam* (width) of most sea kayaks renders unintentional capsizes extremely uncommon. Many, many kayakers paddle their entire careers without ever capsizing, even through major expeditions. Second, if you do capsize, any of several techniques will quickly get you back upright. Most people can learn to Eskimo-roll in an afternoon with competent instruction. Even if you find yourself out of the boat after a capsize (what we call a wet exit), it's possible to be back in the kayak and paddling again within a couple of minutes.

Still, make no mistake—although thousands of paddlers in traditional-style sea kayaks head out to sea with no self-rescue skills at all and manage to avoid trouble, they are being foolish. It's like driving a car with no idea of how to manage a skid or perform an emergency avoidance maneuver. If you decide on a traditional kayak, you'll be a much better, safer, and more confident paddler if you practice rescue and self-recovery techniques, as detailed in chapter 4.

Throughout this book virtually all the techniques I'll discuss will be oriented toward enclosed-cockpit kayaks, since it is much easier to modify these to suit an open-cockpit design than vice versa.

SINGLE VERSUS DOUBLE

For a couple contemplating sea kayaking, a common dilemma is whether to buy two single kayaks or one double. Trust me on this— try a double before you buy one. Even if you're Ozzie and Harriet

A double kayak costs less than two singles, and promotes togetherness—
sometimes!

on shore, things change at sea when you're required to coordinate
your efforts, and when only one of you has directional control (via
the rudder pedals). I've witnessed couples who had never had so
much as a tiff head back to shore spouting visible steam after 15
minutes in a double. Others, of course, were thoroughly entranced
by the experience. Never have I figured out how to predict in
advance which will occur.

Double kayaks have several advantages over singles, and several drawbacks as well. On the positive side, a double kayak costs
less than two singles—although, as I've warned many couples, two
singles cost much less than a typical divorce. Doubles can inspire
confidence in novices, both because it can be nice to have someone else in the boat to communicate with, and because the extra
beam of a double kayak makes it more resistant (but not immune!)
to capsizing. If you do manage to capsize a double, it's generally
easy for you and your partner to help each other reenter the boat;
one can stabilize the craft while the other climbs back in.

One of the best characteristics of double kayaks is that they
tend to equalize the strengths of the paddlers. If one strong and

one weak paddler are together in a double, their efforts will complement each other. If the same two paddlers were in separate boats, the weaker person would constantly lag behind.

Finally, almost any double kayak is faster than almost any single, since you have two people powering one boat. (There are also hydrodynamic reasons for this, which I'll discuss in Design and Dimensions, page 22.) Two people in a double can comfortably cover probably 25 to 35 percent more distance than they would in two singles in the same time.

Naturally, there's a flip side. Double kayaks usually weigh close to 90 pounds; they can be a pain to carry or hoist on top of a roof rack. Dealing with two 60-pound singles is often easier. Of course, if one of you wants to go paddling alone, you're out of luck if you own a double (although it's possible for one person to paddle a double, it is *no* fun, especially with no one in the front cockpit to keep the bow level). And sometimes, even if you're out together, it's nice to separate and explore on your own for a while. Finally, a double kayak usually holds less cargo than two singles, something to keep in mind if you plan extended trips.

An important design characteristic of a double kayak is the distance between the cockpits. If they're close together, the paddlers must synchronize their paddling to avoid whacking the paddles together. Since some interference is inevitable, and you're often dealing with $400 worth of paddles ($200 times two), this is yet another source of discord. In doubles with a center storage compartment (a nice feature in itself), the cockpits are farther apart, so synchronized paddling isn't necessary.

RIGID-HULL VERSUS FOLDING KAYAKS

If your kayaking dreams include travel to the far ends of the earth by commercial airliner, consider buying a folding kayak, which can be collapsed into one or two duffel bags and checked onto any airline as excess baggage (or stored in a closet if you live in a small apartment). At your launch site, it takes less than 30 minutes to assemble a seaworthy craft.

Oddly, commercial folding kayaks have been around far longer than their rigid-hull fiberglass counterparts. The German company Klepper has been making them since the turn of the century; their current Aerius models have changed little in 40 years.

Many couples prefer the freedom and extra gear capacity afforded by two single kayaks.

The Klepper is a beautiful craft, made with gleaming, varnished ash and birch frame pieces and a cotton-canvas deck bonded to a tough Hypalon hull. The French Nautiraid is similar, although the quality is not as high (nor is the price).

In contrast to the traditional approach, the Canadian company Feathercraft went high-tech with its folding kayaks. The frame members are anodized aluminum and high-density polyethylene; the deck is nylon Cordura over a Hypalon hull. Surprisingly, there is little difference in performance between the two construction techniques. Feathercraft's boats seem to be a bit lighter, but even that's hard to quantify since the European boats are short and wide while the Feathercrafts are longer and narrower. The choice between the two styles is really a matter of personal preference.

Folding kayaks—at least the top models, such as Klepper and Feathercraft—are *expensive:* around $4,000 for a new single as I write this. They will, however, last a long time with care, and hold

The beautiful, varnished frame of a Klepper folding kayak.

their value well. When the skin finally wears out you can replace it, rather than having to buy a whole new boat (although the price of just the skin is about the same as that of a new fiberglass kayak).

Besides price, folding kayaks have a couple of disadvantages. Since they have no watertight cargo compartments, you must rely completely on dry bags for both flotation and gear protection

The Feathercraft expedition kayak can fly anywhere in the world as excess baggage.

(most folders incorporate inflatable tubes along the sides, called *sponsons*, which stiffen the structure and provide a little flotation; they are not adequate for safety, however). The numerous frame members are subject to breakage—although field repairs are usually possible—and they intrude on storage space. Finally, folding kayaks are not quite as efficient as their hard-shell counterparts, even though die-hard folder fans would have you think otherwise. The flexible frame inevitably absorbs some of the paddler's energy (just like a too-flexible frame on a bicycle), and the rubber skin stretched over an angular frame is not as slick as a smooth fiberglass hull. Remember, however, that at typical touring speeds this discrepancy is not great; in fact, none of the folder's disadvantages should preclude your buying one if you want to travel abroad with your kayak.

If your launch sites are within driving range and you have the storage space, you will almost certainly prefer the lower cost, greater efficiency, increased safety, and more generous storage space of a hard-shell kayak. Depending on materials, a hard-shell kayak costs from one-third to one-half what a top-quality folding boat does. The stiff hull and sleek surface ensure good performance, and storage compartments keep gear dry and provide flotation. And note that it's perfectly possible to fly anywhere in the world with a rigid-hull boat, but it will be classified as freight rather than baggage and the cost will be far higher.

MATERIALS

Unless you're a lot wealthier than, say, the average outdoor writer, the material of which your kayak is constructed will probably be determined by your budget. That's because the various materials—plastic, fiberglass, Kevlar—escalate in that order in both performance and price. The more you spend, the more performance you get. (Performance, in this context, refers to several things: durability, longevity, hydrodynamic efficiency, and looks.)

Plastic

Most plastic kayaks are made from rotomolded polyethylene. The polyethylene is poured in beads into a huge, heated kayak-shaped mold, which slowly revolves (hence the term *rotomolded*), melting and distributing the plastic in a more or less even film over the inner surface. The mold is then cooled and opened, and out pops a sea kayak.

Polyethylene kayaks are relatively inexpensive—fully equipped examples are running between $1,000 and $1,400 as I write this—and tough. You can bounce them off rocks with apparent impunity; I've even heard of plastic boats getting blown off roof racks on the freeway and surviving with nothing to show but a few gouges.

But polyethylene has significant disadvantages as well. While the material is resistant to impact, if you abuse it by dragging the boat over rocks or reefs the hull will abrade, raising a "fuzz" that adds drag beneath the waterline. Polyethylene is subject to ultraviolet deterioration and, even with care, has a definite life span, after which it will begin to turn brittle (this can range from less than 5 years to 10 or so). Polyethylene kayaks are heavier than fiberglass models, yet less rigid—many require reinforcing struts along the keel to prevent the boat from flexing too much. The material can also take a set, or warp, if the boat is stored improperly or cinched down too tightly on a roof rack. When this happens the hull can bend out of true, greatly affecting the handling of the boat until the material slowly resets itself. If holed or split, polyethylene is difficult to repair, because few adhesives bond well to it.

Aesthetics are subjective. Since polyethylene kayaks come from a one-piece mold, they inevitably suffer from a sort of squeezed-from-a-tube look, and the plastic has little natural gloss or character. There's certainly nothing in the way of craftsmanship to be found in a plastic boat. At least the color is molded in, so scratches don't stand out.

The two most common forms of polyethylene are *linear* and *cross-linked;* the terms refer to the way the polymer molecules are aligned. Cross-linked polyethylene is touted as stronger than linear, but it cannot be recycled—when its useful life span is over, the kayak is 60 pounds of garbage. Linear polyethylene can be reused to make secondary items such as hatch covers and seats. However, even this usefulness is at the mercy of the market—sometimes it's cheaper for manufacturers to use new material than to recycle old boats. Perhaps someday we'll recycle such materials not because it's cheaper, but because it's the right thing to do.

Another type of plastic is the HTP marketed by a manufacturer called Prijon (pronounced PREE-yon). HTP is blow-molded—formed in presses—rather than rotomolded. Prijon claims it's stiffer than rotomolded plastic; it's also 100 percent recyclable—that is, the material in an old boat can be melted down and used to make a new one.

A further development in plastic kayaks could prove to be the best yet. Eddyline Kayaks was the first company to produce a kayak made from a polycarbonate alloy, similar to the stuff in ski goggle lenses. It's quite stiff—much stiffer than polyethylene—and more resistant to scratches and gouges. Eddyline says its accelerated-wear tests show the polycarbonate to be more resistant to ultraviolet deterioration as well. The material comes in sheets that are vacuum-molded by essentially sucking them down into separate hull- and deck-shaped molds, then joined along a seam. This allows the deck to be a contrasting color to the hull, avoiding the monochrome appearance of polyethylene boats. The cost of polycarbonate, as you might expect, is higher than polyethylene, but lower than fiberglass.

My basic advice on plastic kayaks is this: While polyethylene is far from a perfect material, keep in mind that a rotomolded kayak will go anywhere any other kayak will. If your budget dictates, don't hesitate to choose one. If you're unsure, however, think about this: I've known dozens of people who bought plastic kayaks and later traded them in for fiberglass models, but no one who bought fiberglass and later traded for plastic. As technology advances—particularly with innovations such as polycarbonate—the performance and aesthetic gaps between fiberglass and plastic boats will likely diminish.

Fiberglass

Simply put, fiberglass is a nearly perfect material with which to make sea kayaks. It is very strong for its weight and has a virtually unlimited life span—some of the first fiberglass sailboats, built nearly 50 years ago, are still sailing. The glossy exterior coating of a fiberglass kayak, called gelcoat, looks beautiful and produces very little friction against the water. Fiberglass kayaks are stiff enough to need no additional reinforcement.

Fiberglass boats are tough. Dragging one over rocks will scratch the gelcoat on the hull, but do little to degrade performance. You can stand on the decks of most fiberglass kayaks without hurting them. And while fiberglass isn't generally as forgiving of severe rock impacts as plastic, if you do manage to put a hole in a fiberglass boat it can be easily repaired in the field with nothing more than duct tape, and repaired permanently at home later.

Of course, fiberglass costs a little more. Fiberglass single kayaks run from around $1,800 to $2,500 or so. That extra cost is more than made up for in the long run with a more durable, better-performing boat that will command a higher price on the used market.

The procedure by which a fiberglass boat is built is called the *layup*. Fiberglass (also known as FRP, for Fiber-Reinforced Plastic), normally comes in a clothlike woven material for use in kayaks. The material is laid into separate molds for hull and deck after the gelcoat is sprayed in, then the cloth is saturated with resin, which hardens the cloth to a stiff, but slightly flexible, unit. Finally, the hull and deck are bonded together along the center seam. In general, the finer the weave of cloth used in the boat, the lighter the boat can be made while retaining good strength. You can see the weave of the fiberglass cloth by looking inside the cockpit or cargo holds of the kayak, and compare it with other models.

Another, cheaper way to build fiberglass boats (usually inexpensive sailboats) is with chopped strands of fiberglass, which are sprayed from a gun into the mold, resulting in a heavier and less flexible structure. I'm not aware of any kayaks being built this way, but if I found one I wouldn't buy it (you can easily spot the short, random strands of material in the layup of a boat built with sprayed strand).

The hull and deck of the kayak can be joined in two ways. Most manufacturers use an extruded-seam strip—an I-beam-shaped strip of plastic into which the hull and deck are glued, after which a fiberglass strip is laid along the inside. A few makers eschew the plastic strip and use only fiberglass to bond the two pieces; this is more difficult but theoretically stronger. However, I've only heard of one extruded-seam boat coming apart, and I wouldn't hesitate to buy a kayak made either way.

One of the advantages to building with fiberglass is that the material can be molded into very precise shapes. This allows designers to fine-tune hull characteristics beyond what is possible with a rotomolded design. I've paddled kayak designs that were available in both fiberglass and polyethylene; the fiberglass boat always felt just a bit sharper-handling. Of course, it's possible that this perception was just my built-in prejudice; it would be interesting to paddle the same boats disguised so I couldn't tell which was which by looking, and see if I could still discern a difference in personality.

Kevlar

Kevlar is the DuPont trademark name for aramid (*aromatic poly*amide) fiber, an astoundingly strong synthetic. Kevlar is even stronger than fiberglass; kayaks made from it can be lighter than their fiberglass equivalents while maintaining similar or even superior strength. The material comes in a fine-weave cloth and is laid up very similarly to fiberglass. The kayaks are often finished with a clear gelcoat to show off the golden hues of the Kevlar beneath.

The downside to Kevlar is its cost-benefit ratio. Because a lot of the weight of a fiberglass or Kevlar boat is in the resin, a kayak made with 100 percent Kevlar might be 10 percent lighter than a similar fiberglass boat—say 50 pounds, instead of 55 or 56—but it will cost about $400 to $500 more. The weight savings is handy when you're carrying the boat or loading and unloading it from the car, but it becomes insignificant when the boat is in the water with your 110 or 160 pounds inside—even more so if you add camping gear. Unless you're on an unrestricted budget, I suggest putting that extra money into lighter *paddles,* which will gain you more real performance.

OTHER FEATURES

Bulkheads

If you're looking at a traditional kayak, make sure it has waterproof bulkheads both behind and in front of the cockpit. These bulkheads provide flotation in the ends of the boat in the unlikely event your kayak is capsized and the cockpit fills with water. A kayak with twin bulkheads is nearly impossible to sink, even if both compartments are packed with gear.

Some older kayaks, and a very few cheap new ones, have only a rear bulkhead, forcing you to use flotation bags in the bow. Not only is this awkward, but the bags could conceivably come loose after a rough capsize. If this happens, the bow of the kayak will sink while the stern floats; the whole boat winds up sticking straight up in the air, making recovery almost impossible. It's just not worth the risk—insist on double bulkheads.

Bulkheads in fiberglass kayaks can be made from fiberglass, or they can be high-density foam. I think fiberglass is much better, since it's bonded to the hull and becomes part of the structure. Foam bulkheads must be caulked to the hull with adhesive, and are much more likely to leak or come completely loose. Unfortunately, foam bulkheads are becoming the norm, probably because they're easier to install. If you buy a kayak equipped with foam bulkheads, keep a close eye on them. The minute they begin to exhibit signs of leakage or looseness, recaulk them with a big, ugly bead of butyl rubber sealant.

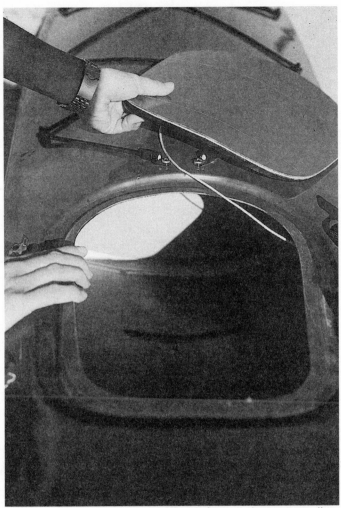

Make sure your kayak has bulkheads front and rear, as well as secure cargo hatches.

Bulkheads in plastic kayaks are usually foam, too, with the added complication that most adhesives bond poorly to polyethylene. Molded-plastic bulkheads are the answer; they can be plastic-welded to the hull, resulting in a very strong bond. Dagger and Valley Canoe both use plastic bulkheads; hopefully others will follow.

Of course, if you're buying a folding kayak you'll have no bulkheads at all, since no one has yet figured out a way to incorporate them into a folder. Fortunately, it's easy to secure flotation bags (or dry bags filled with gear, which are very buoyant) inside a folding kayak by running straps around the frame members in front of the bags. It's not as good as watertight compartments, but will keep the boat afloat.

Hatch Covers

Hatch covers should be large enough to facilitate easy loading, but not so big that they flex or distort—or pop off—under heavy waves. On fiberglass kayaks, covers made from the same material and layup as the deck are the best, with good thick molded-plastic versions second (plastic kayaks will, of course, have plastic covers). Check the rear cover particularly; on some boats these are made way too big. If you can easily invert the cover by pressing on it with your palm, imagine what several hundred pounds of water in a big wave will do.

The closer to flush the covers are to the deck, the less spray they will throw into your face in rough weather, the less force waves can exert on them, and the less likely they are to leak. Most hatch covers are secured with two straps; I like having three for redundancy. It should be easy for the manufacturer to add another if you ask. If not, you can do it yourself.

Actually, the best hatch covers I've found take no straps at all. They are made from heavy rubber and fit like a Tupperware lid over the hatch coaming. Valley Canoe Products in England pioneered these in a ridiculously small, 7-inch-diameter size, which was fiendishly difficult to load through; the 10-inch versions are much better, and the newer oval style is the best yet—secure and very watertight, yet offering excellent gear access. Kajak Sport makes similar models. Actually, the only problem I've found with some of these covers is that they seal *too* well—on a hot day, when the air inside the kayak expands, I've seen rubber covers bulge like an incipient volcano, threatening to blow right off. The solution is a tiny, $\frac{1}{64}$-inch hole drilled through the bulkhead right under the deck. This is large enough to bleed off excess pressure but not to cause noticeable leakage if the craft is capsized.

Incidentally, some kayaks—mostly British models, but more and more American counterparts as well—are available with a third watertight compartment just behind the cockpit. An additional hatch allows you to access the compartment while paddling. I think these are wonderful for safe storage of items you might want on the water; they help limit deck clutter and reduce the chances of your snack bag or water bottle—or camera—being washed overboard. Their only drawback is the awkward reach behind you and the blind groping to locate the desired object, complicated further if the weather is rough.

Deck Rigging

If you buy an "expedition-equipped" kayak, it will likely have a bunch of bungees and cleats and stuff riveted to the deck. The bungees in front of the cockpit are handy for securing items you might want or need during a paddle—a paddle float (see chapter 2, page 42), a deck bag for small items such as sunscreen, and so on. The rear bungees can be used to stash the jacket that gets too warm late in the morning. Keep in mind that anything you secure with deck bungees is, first, sure to get soaked, and, second, subject to being lost overboard if it's not secured with a safety line. Also keep in mind that the deck is no place to store heavy or bulky gear that won't fit inside the boat; you will upset your center of gravity and increase windage significantly.

The bungees are also used to carry your spare paddle, usually on the rear deck. Some companies are adding additional, smaller bungee loops farther back on the deck. These are to secure the shafts of the (two-piece) paddle, while the blades go under the bungees just behind the cockpit. This combination helps ensure against the paddle getting washed overboard, while still making retrieval easy.

Many American kayaks are equipped with two cleats just in front of the cockpit. These are great for tying off a bowline or securing safety lines for other deck items, but the cleats are also referred to as a "paddle park." If you rest your paddle shaft across the cleats, perpendicular to the boat, you can pull a loop of deck bungee over the shaft and hook it under the rear noses of the cleats, securing the paddle temporarily while you do other things. It works well in calm conditions, but in rough water the paddle blades can plunge beneath the surface and yank the whole thing loose.

Deck bungees are useful for securing frequently needed items.

The bow and stern toggles are your handles for carrying the kayak. They usually have a piece of PVC pipe threaded through them for a more comfortable grip. I've only run into a few that were poorly placed—mostly in the stern, where the rudder assembly can interfere with knuckle or thigh clearance.

Some American manufacturers are incorporating a useful English innovation: perimeter lines. These are nonelastic lines running through fittings—usually recessed into the deck—around the perimeter of the deck. They're designed to serve as handholds if you're assisting another kayaker who has capsized and is in the water, or if you've capsized yourself. You still don't find them on many boats (except British models), but they're a nice feature to have.

Paddle Float Rigging

More manufacturers are now building in a rigging system to secure a paddle firmly across the rear deck for a *paddle float rescue* (see chapter 4, page 89). This is a great idea; for too long the deck bungees were pressed into service for this task, and bungees are far too elastic to properly secure the paddle shaft. Nylon straps are much preferable. A few models even incorporate a groove molded across the deck to really anchor the shaft.

Compass

Even if you have no intention of ever undertaking an expedition, a compass is a good addition to your kayak. Along with its usefulness as a safety device—especially if night or fog catches you far from home—a compass is great for pointing out things of interest to your fellow paddlers, simply by telling them along what bearing to look.

I prefer a compass mounted fairly far forward on deck, just behind or on top of the front hatch cover. In this position you don't have to drop your eyes as far to check the heading as you do with an instrument mounted right in front of the cockpit; also, the latter position will interfere with storage of incidental items under the deck bungees, and will be completely covered if you mount a deck bag.

Color

A brighter kayak is a safer kayak. Not only can powerboats and sailors spot you from farther away, but so can rescue personnel if

A deck-mounted compass is essential if you plan on touring with your kayak.

the need ever arises. Yellow and red have been proven to show up the best in all conditions, followed by orange and bright purple.

The problem, of course, is that it would be a dull world if we all paddled yellow or red kayaks, so I don't expect the broad palettes offered by our kayak makers to diminish anytime soon. Also, keep in mind that even the brightest kayak disappears from a few hundred yards away, so for real safety you need other signaling devices (see chapter 2, page 46).

One thing I do recommend on a fiberglass boat, no matter what deck color you choose, is a white or off-white hull. Scratches are much less noticeable on white hulls, and are easier to repair without having to precisely match the gelcoat.

DESIGN AND DIMENSIONS

You could paddle 10 different kayaks from 10 different manufacturers, each of them exactly 17 feet long and 23 inches wide, and every one of them would have its own personality. One might be easy to turn but very poor at *tracking* (holding a straight course); another could be just the opposite. One might feel tippy at first but seem nearly impossible to capsize; another might seem stable as a raft but have an abrupt point at which it falls right over if you lean too far. There are so many variables in hull design that it's nearly impossible to draw any conclusions as to how a boat will handle just by looking at the measurements. However, although the science of hydrodynamics is complex, the characteristics that give each boat its uniqueness are easy to understand.

There are essentially four qualities that combine to produce the personality of a kayak. In no order of importance, they are:

- Stability
- Tracking (the ability to hold a straight course)
- Maneuverability
- Speed

Let's look at the different design elements of the kayak, and see how they affect these qualities. Keep in mind that it's impossible to separate all these elements conclusively; their individual effects blend to produce a whole.

Length, Keel Design, and Rocker

Most single sea kayaks run between 15 and 19 feet in overall length; doubles can go from 17 to 22 feet. *Overall length* refers to the measurement from the very front of the boat to the very back, but a more important measurement is the *waterline length*. This is the length of the boat at the waterline, always somewhat and sometimes considerably shorter than overall length. Two kayaks of the same overall length might have waterline lengths that differ by a foot or more.

In general, the longer the waterline length, the better the kayak will track—that is, the better it will hold a straight course (especially in wind and waves) without requiring you to make constant corrections. On the other hand, a kayak with a shorter waterline length will generally turn quicker, making it more maneuverable, but will require more attention to hold a course on long, straight crossings.

Tracking and turning are also affected by the *keel* of the kayak—the line running down the middle of the hull from bow to stern. Some kayaks have a visible ridge along the keel, which enhances tracking and slows turning. On a kayak with a more rounded hull, the keel line is featureless; only the sharp bow and stern provide "grip" to facilitate tracking.

Another factor in this equation is the *rocker* of the hull. If you look at a kayak from the side as it's sitting on a flat surface, the center of the boat will obviously be in contact, but the bow and stern will be raised to a greater or lesser degree. If the ends are well off the ground, the hull has significant rocker. A boat with a lot of rocker tends to turn quicker—at the expense of tracking, since with the ends of the boat out of the water the whole thing functions as a shorter craft. However, putting a load in the boat lowers it in the water and submerges more of the ends, enhancing tracking.

Back to length. Theoretically, a longer kayak will also be faster than a short one—but theory collides somewhat with reality here.

As a kayak (any boat, in fact) moves through the water, it creates two waves, a bow wave and a stern wave. As the boat moves faster, those waves get bigger and harder to push. At a certain speed the boat essentially gets sucked down into the trough of its own waves, and paddling harder will result in little or no increase in speed. The farther apart the bow and stern waves are, the faster they can be pushed, but eventually the boat hits a "wall," known as the *hull speed* of the craft. Theoretical hull speed can be figured in knots by multiplying the square root of the boat's waterline length by 1.34. For example, a kayak 16 feet at the waterline has a hull speed of 4×1.34, or 5.36 knots, or about 6.2 miles per hour (a knot equals 1.15 miles per hour). So a longer kayak will have a higher hull speed than a shorter kayak. Hull speed can be exceeded under certain circumstances—that's why it's called "theoretical"—but it provides a reasonable comparison between boats. (One way to far exceed it, by the way, is with a hull designed to plane on the surface of the water, like a speedboat, but that's out of the question for a kayaker.)

The problem is this: A higher hull speed is only attainable when you're paddling at maximum effort, which is rarely the case when touring. At lower speeds another factor plays a more important role—the *wetted surface* of the hull, which is the actual area of the hull that's submerged and producing friction against the water. At hull speed, this friction constitutes only about 40 percent of the resistance; the bow and stern waves account for the other 60 percent. However, at 3.5 knots—roughly 4 miles per hour, a normal touring pace—the wetted surface friction constitutes a full 85 percent of the total resistance, since at that speed the bow and stern waves are very small. What this means is that, at a normal cruising speed, a kayak with a small wetted surface might take less energy to move than one with a longer waterline and a theoretically higher top speed.

If all this is beginning to sound complicated, keep one very important point in mind: Tests have shown that at a typical touring pace, there's very little difference between most kayak models in terms of resistance and speed. Unless you plan to race your kayak, you're far better off concentrating on its fit and its relation to your own size than on any preconceived dogma regarding what's faster or slower.

Beam and Cross Section

The beam, or width, of the kayak is the most easily distinguishable design variable from the perspective of the cockpit. A novice who tries a 24-inch-wide kayak will almost certainly prefer it to a 22-inch-wide model, since, all else being equal, the wider boat will feel much more stable. On the other hand, many experts will tell you a kayak *has* to be narrow to be seaworthy. Neither perception is entirely true.

Kayakers talk about two kinds of stability. *Initial stability* is what you feel when you first sit in the boat in the water—the degree to which the boat rocks back and forth when you wiggle your hips. *Final stability,* the more ominous-sounding term, is the point at which, if you continue to lean your whole body sideways, the kayak capsizes. And I specify *lean your whole body* because it's possible to lean *just* the kayak while keeping your torso upright. Keep this in mind; it's a vital facet of boat control you'll learn more about a little later.

Initial and final stability are not always correlated. One kayak might feel very stable at first, but capsize with little warning if a critical angle is exceeded. Another model might feel tippy initially, but get firmer and firmer the more you lean.

To be both seaworthy and comfortable a kayak must be stable enough that you can look around, take photographs, or examine a chart in your lap without feeling like you might inadvertently capsize.

On the other hand, you must be able to use body English to rock the kayak to compensate for wave motion, especially if seas are coming from the side (abeam). If the kayak is too wide it will feel very stable in small waves, but as conditions get rougher the kayak will tilt to ride up the side of the waves, throwing you more and more off balance. In a narrower boat you can use simple hip movements to keep the kayak level with the horizon while the waves just roll by, a compensation that becomes utterly instinctive with practice.

This combination of intrinsic stability and, shall we say, "rockability" is the key to a seaworthy kayak. For most paddlers, the two come together somewhere in the 22- to 24-inch range of beam. A 6-foot-tall, 180-pound male will likely want something toward the wide end of the scale, while a 5-foot-2, 105-pound female might feel just as stable in a narrower model, and be able to control it much more effectively.

Almost as important as the beam to the feel of the kayak is the cross-sectional shape of the hull. A kayak with *hard chines*—that is, a noticeable "corner" where the bottom of the hull curves up to the sides—and a shallow V-shaped bottom will usually have a lot of initial stability; in fact, some models feel almost raftlike. I've found, however, that hard-chine boats seem to have a slightly more abrupt point at which a capsize feels imminent. That's not necessarily bad, just different. A kayak with a bottom shaped like a flattened bowl will feel tippier initially—the slightest movement of your hips will cause it to rock. But as you lean the boat farther and farther, it resists more and more. The least-stable shape is almost semicircular, and is usually only found on very narrow Greenland-style kayaks or high-performance racing craft.

Volume and Volume Placement

You might think that the volume of a kayak is simply a measure of how much gear it will hold, but volume—and the placement of it—has a significant effect on the handling of the boat.

A kayak with most of its volume near the cockpit, with very narrow ("fine" in nautical terms) ends, tends to track very well, while still turning decently if the boat is leaned while turning (see chapter 3, page 74). The fine ends also allow the kayak to cut through small waves instead of bouncing over them, making for a smoother ride in small seas. This configuration is common on British designs.

RUDDERS AND SKEGS As you might have already guessed, it's almost impossible to design a kayak that will both track well and turn quickly when desired. So most modern sea kayaks employ a movable device, either a rudder or skeg, to help.

A *rudder* is a foot-controlled blade that helps both tracking and turning. To turn, you simply push the pedal that corresponds to the direction you want to go—right to turn right, left for left. When held centered, the rudder also helps the boat maintain a straight course; you can also cant it just a bit to compensate for wind-induced wandering. It can be raised out of the water for launching and landing, or when you want to paddle without it.

A *skeg* is like the centerboard on a sailboat. It fits up in a slot near the stern, and is lowered straight down with a cable. Since a skeg doesn't pivot side to side, it functions solely as a tracking aid; turning is left to hull design and the skill of the paddler.

Skegs are common on British kayaks; in fact, the British still tend to view rudders with no little disdain, believing them to be too often used as a substitute for good paddling skills. And they're right—many Americans rely completely on their rudders for boat control, and are virtually helpless if a cable breaks in rough conditions. If your kayak has a rudder you should practice as often as possible with it retracted, and not just when it's calm.

With this in mind, however, the rudder is certainly the more versatile of the two devices, and easier for a novice to master. The team of English- men—very experienced paddlers all—who first circumnavigated the British Isles used British kayaks retrofitted with foot-controlled rudders.

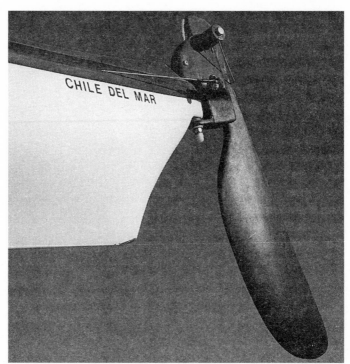
A rudder assists both tracking and turning on many kayaks.

The problem with fine ends is that they also tend to cut through *big* waves, sending water over the deck and sometimes into the chest of the paddler, and they greatly restrict the amount of cargo space in the ends of the boat. A kayak with "fuller" ends, while admittedly a bit bouncy in small waves, will be more likely to ride over big ones, and will hold more gear. In addition, a fuller bow and stern can increase the final stability of a kayak compared to one of identical maximum beam but finer ends. (On a minor technical note, very fine ends can sometimes move the bow wave back along the boat's hull, reducing effective waterline length and lowering the theoretical hull speed. I doubt this would be notice-able to a touring paddler, however.)

NARROWING THE FIELD

Now you know enough about sea-kayak design to start analyzing your needs and narrowing the choices you'll be faced with when you go shopping.

The majority of single sea-kayak designs fall between 16 and 18 feet in length, which is a good compromise among tracking, maneuverability, and gear space. If your kayaking plans include multiday trips for which you'll need a significant amount of gear, I recommend staying close to those measurements. If you're very large or are considering really epic expeditions, you can go longer, with an 18- or 18 $\frac{1}{2}$-foot boat; if you're short, you might consider something a little shorter than 16 feet.

If you're certain your paddling will be mostly restricted to day trips, you might want a substantially shorter boat, in the 14- to 15-foot range. The boat will be lighter (easier to carry) and more maneuverable. You'll lose a bit of speed, but it's doubtful you'll ever notice. And there's still plenty of room for overnight or week-end trips, and even longer ones if you pack carefully.

Beam is a little more subjective. It's hard to predict how comfortable you'll be with a particular design, even after you've paddled it once or twice. Generally, however, that 22- to 24-inch span is a good guide. Almost anything narrower than this will feel pretty insecure to a beginner (heck, most skinny boats feel insecure to me, too). If you buy your clothes at big-and-tall stores you can go wider—Pacific Water Sports, for example, makes a model called the Thunderbird specifically targeted at paddlers well over 200 pounds; it's 27 inches wide. Also note aberrations such as the folding Klepper Aerius, which is 15 feet long and 27 inches wide, but intended for average-size paddlers.

If you're in the market for a double, the parameters are a bit looser. That's mostly because it's hard to tailor the fit of a double kayak perfectly to both paddlers. So your external needs will play a greater role.

If you plan on touring I suggest a double with a center storage compartment, for three reasons. First, gear space is vastly increased with a center compartment. Second, you get an extra flotation chamber for safety's sake. The center bulkheads also prevent water from sloshing back and forth between the two cockpits if you're ever swamped. Finally, the extra distance between the cockpits means you and your partner don't have to coordinate your paddles to avoid whacking them together. Doubles with center compartments usually run between 21 and 22 $\frac{1}{2}$ feet in length.

If you're interested in day trips or a more maneuverable boat, you can skip the center compartment, which will shorten overall length by a couple of feet. You'll have to practice synchronizing your paddle strokes, though.

Remember not to cast your guidelines in stone. Every kayak will feel different, and it's important to get the one that feels right for you.

THE TEST DRIVE

So far the decisions you've made could have been done from your living room. Now it's time to try some boats.

As a beginner, testing a kayak presents an obvious problem—you have no frame of reference by which to judge what you're experiencing. You might think it's like asking a 16-year-old with a learner's permit to decide which is better—a Porsche Carrera or a Ferrari F355 (now, there's a scary scenario). But there are many facets to kayak design for which even a newcomer can quickly develop a feel.

Since you've already decided on the type of kayak you want—say, a fiberglass single about 17 feet long and 23 to 24 inches in beam—you should be able to narrow your choices to no more than three or four kayaks per dealer. At this point, don't hesitate to choose candidates based on the style that catches your eye. One of the most vital facets of sea kayaking is the grace intrinsic to the craft. You'll paddle a beautiful boat better than you will an ugly one. Trust me.

Once a particular kayak has attracted you, the first, and by far most important, judgment to make involves fit and comfort. You can get a decent idea of this just sitting in the boat in the showroom while you're talking to the salesclerk or reading the brochure. The seat should feel comfortable right off the bat—if it doesn't, it's highly unlikely to improve if you sit in it longer. Adjust the rudder pedals so you can comfortably operate them. You should be able to brace your knees under the deck while simultaneously working the rudder; this is vital in rough water to allow you to control the boat with body English. The cockpit should feel snug but not confining. If anything feels awkward, try another boat.

The more adjustments the seat has available, the better. Sometimes it's nice to be able to shift your posture strictly for variety's sake, even if the seat is perfectly comfortable, but if your trips range from a paddle in warm water with light clothing to well-clothed journeys in the Arctic, it's essential to be able to vary the seat back. The bottom of the seat should be right on the floor of the kayak, or very close to it. I once had a kayak with a seat mounted a good inch off the bottom, which I redrilled to a lower position. The stability of the kayak immediately improved—just that inch made a difference. That's why I don't like to pad uncomfortable seats—all this does is raise the center of gravity.

Check how easy it is to get out of the cockpit. If you can lift your knees out of the cockpit while you're sitting, you shouldn't have any trouble exiting quickly in the water. If you can't lift your knees out, make sure you can slide backward out of the cockpit by putting your hands on each side of the cockpit rim, lifting your rear out of the seat, and sliding out onto the rear deck. Many British kayaks have tight cockpits that require this movement to exit; the British don't like big cockpit openings, because they feel a large spray skirt can more easily pop off in heavy weather. (I think that's only a danger with cheap spray skirts; see chapter 2).

Unlike many other sports, it's perfectly possible for a rank beginner to climb into a sea kayak and make reasonable progress paddling around a sheltered harbor or bay. Many kayak shops sponsor "demo days" to give prospective customers the opportunity to paddle several different boats; other on-the-water stores have demo kayaks available at any time. Sometimes employees are available to offer advice and basic instruction.

It's nice to be able to try a kayak next to a low dock, so you can sit in the boat while hanging on to the platform. This will give you a chance to see how the boat feels; you can rock back and forth and lean while staying secure and not worrying about tipping over. Don't be surprised if the kayak feels tippy at first; after all, this is a very unfamiliar craft to you. Keep your grip on the dock while you rock back and forth, then try leaning in one direction until the boat feels as though it's ready to capsize. This is easier to detect than you might think—as you begin to lean, the boat will resist tipping more and more, but you'll reach a point, usually quite noticeable, when the resistance falls off quickly and the boat "wants" to tip. Most beginners are surprised at how far you can lean a sea kayak before it tries to capsize. If you keep your torso upright and just lean the boat with your hips, you can easily dunk the cockpit rim in the water.

If you read through part 2 of this book first, you'll be able to paddle around the harbor with little fuss or nervousness. Pay attention to how the kayak feels once you've gotten used to the initial strangeness. It should be responsive to your hip movements, but you should be able to look around or take photos without feeling like you're in imminent danger of falling over. If you just can't get over the tippy feeling, try a slightly wider model, or one with a different hull shape. Keep in mind that if you plan on touring in the boat, it will actually be more stable with a full load than when empty. In fact, I wouldn't hesitate to ask the staff for some weight to add to the compartments.

In the end, one kayak almost always speaks louder than the others. Listen to it.

CHAPTER 2

OTHER EQUIPMENT

After deciding on the centerpiece of your sea-kayaking equipment, it can be hard to concentrate on what seem like ancillary purchases. In fact, it would be worth taking the boat home, installing it in the living room or garage, and just admiring it for a few days before heading back to buy the rest of your gear. But you probably want to go paddling. So shake your head and try to focus. Remember that the kayak must function smoothly as a unit for you to get the most out of the experience, so it's important to take just as much care with your accessories as you did with your boat.

PADDLE

If you told me you had exactly $1,000, and not a penny more, to spend between your sea kayak and paddles, I'd tell you to buy a good used rotomolded plastic kayak for $500, and spend the other $500 on two of the best paddles you could find. That's how important the paddle is to your kayaking performance.

The paddle represents weight you must constantly hold up, swing, and maneuver. The lighter it is, the better. Yet it must also be very strong. When you brace with the paddle it is subject to significant stress, and when used for a paddle float rescue it must support nearly your whole weight. To combine light weight and sufficient strength requires top-quality materials and careful construction.

Buy the best paddles you can afford.

Quality paddles can be made from either wood laminates or synthetic materials such as fiberglass, carbon fiber, or graphite (which is a form of carbon; the two terms are sometimes used interchangeably).

Wood paddles are very serviceable and a delight to look at. Most good ones weigh under 40 ounces, which I consider to be about the upper end of reasonable paddle weight. Wood paddles tend to cost a bit less than synthetic models (about $120 to $200)—except for the really fancy ones with intricate laminations or inlays of dolphins and whales. Properly made wood paddles are very strong and have a long service life given an occasional revarnishing. An intact finish on wood paddles is vital, because if water gets into the wood itself the fibers will start to degrade quickly. Many good wood paddles have blade tips of solid fiberglass, since this is where the majority of abrasion occurs. Other areas still need to be watched closely, however.

The advantage of synthetic paddles is that the designer can specify how much material to apply in each area, precisely balancing weight and strength. A good hand-laid (as opposed to pressure-molded) fiberglass paddle will weigh a very reasonable 35 ounces or so and be immensely strong and virtually maintenance-free, aside from an occasional lube of the joint. If you've got the money, you can buy an all-graphite model that weighs no more than 25 ounces, sometimes even less. Such featherweight wands are a delight to use and are still perfectly strong, although definitely not as durable for pushing off rocks, with blades no thicker than shirt cardboard. Two-piece fiberglass paddles start at around $150; an all-graphite version will set you back $300 or more. A good compromise is to order a fiberglass shaft with graphite blades; this lowers "swing weight" out at the ends, where it's most important, and saves you $50 or so.

The most important design variable on paddles is the blade width. A wide blade—7 or 8 inches—offers more power with each stroke, and more surface area for bracing and rolling. A narrow 4- or 5-inch blade takes less energy per stroke, making it easier to use all day and reducing the chances of strain injuries; it also catches the wind less. After my first, wide-bladed paddle was nearly blown out of my grasp on a stormy crossing, I switched to narrow paddles and have stuck with them ever since. You can also split the difference with a medium-width blade of 6 inches.

Three paddle blades, showing different widths.

I've never had a problem with bracing or rolling with my narrow blades, although there's no doubt that it requires a little more effort. I've also never noticed a lack of power when I need to sprint out of a rip current or through an offshore break. And, perhaps significantly, I've never suffered from wrist or elbow problems. Still, this is my choice, and—particularly if you're powerfully built—you might prefer a wide paddle.

The overall length of the paddle should be proportional to your own size. The average paddle length is around 230 to 240 centimeters. If you're tall, you might prefer a 250 or even a 260; shorter paddlers will do better with a 220. If you're in doubt, err on the short side. The reason for this is that the farther away from the centerline of the kayak you plant your paddle blades, the more the kayak *yaws*, or weaves from side to side. Those paddling wide double kayaks—28 to 30 inches or more—might need slightly longer paddles to keep from banging them against the side of the boat.

The ideal shape for the blades is a subject of much debate. Some paddles are completely symmetrical—there is no right-way up, or front or back, and you can swap ends and paddle with either blade facing either way. Most blades, though, are assymetrical; the top of the blade is fairly straight, and the bottom edge curves up to meet it. These blades are usually spoon shaped when viewed from above as well, so they have a definite top and bottom *and* front and back. The reports I've read seem to indicate that the assymetrical blades are slightly more efficient at propulsion and reducing "flutter"—the back-and-forth wobbling that sometimes occurs as a paddle is drawn through the water.

It's a little cheaper to buy one-piece paddles, but they're really awkward to store and transport. After I dealt with a one-piece paddle for a couple of years, all my succeeding paddles have been two-piece. You need to keep the joints of fiberglass paddles lubricated with dry graphite, however, or you'll soon be the owner of a one-piece paddle whether you want one or not.

Finally—and this is going to hurt—buy a spare paddle, *of the same quality as your primary one.* You should never, ever launch your kayak without having a spare paddle on deck. And if you ever need the spare, it's likely to be because nasty conditions have taken away or even broken your main paddle, and this is exactly when you don't want to be caught with inferior equipment. So no matter how tempting it might be to economize on number two, don't do it.

The only semi-exception to the above rule is if you've splurged on a graphite paddle. Then it's perfectly acceptable to use a fiberglass equivalent for your spare. In fact, this is my standard setup. I use the lightweight, expensive paddle for long, uninterrupted stretches, and switch to my heavier-duty fiberglass secondary for skirting rocky coasts (where I might want to fend off submerged boulders), or on days when I know I'll be doing a lot of

Always carry a spare paddle, well secured but accessible from the cockpit.

Other Equipment

launchings and landings (fiberglass holds up better for pushing off beaches).

Some people I know also buy one narrow and one wide paddle; that way they can switch as conditions or mood dictates.

If you spend the money for good paddles, spend a bit more and buy a case for them, which will significantly cut down on the number of dings and chunks taken out of the edges of the blades during transport. Besides, a paddle case emblazoned with the manufacturer's logo looks really zooty.

Paddle Leash

Many expert paddlers suggest tying the paddle with a thin cord to either your wrist or the kayak; this way it can't be lost if torn from your grasp by a gust of wind. It's a good idea—especially the wrist version, which offers greater freedom of movement and less chance of tangling. I must admit I don't normally use a paddle leash, just because I don't like having *any* excess line around that could catch on something. However, I do keep a paddle leash coiled on deck at all times; when I need both hands free for a rescue or photography or snacking, I clip in the paddle and let it float next to the boat.

PFD (PERSONAL FLOTATION DEVICE)

PFDs are like seat belts: Everyone knows they should use them, nearly everyone *has* them, and yet far, far too many sea kayakers are found drowned next to their boats, their PFDs still strapped securely to the rear deck—just as the newspapers tell us of corpses lying on the highway, their seat belts unbuckled in the wrecked car behind them.

Did I get your attention? I hope so. The fact is, sea kayaking is statistically one of the safest outdoor sports in the world. The very few tragic accidents that occur each year almost invariably result from one of two choices made by the paddlers: not to wear a PFD, or not to wear proper clothing to prevent immersion hypothermia (about which more late; see page 51).

Wear a PFD anytime you get in your kayak; it's just plain stupid not to. You can buy a top-quality PFD for $60; even the fanciest imported models are less than $200. I think the most comfortable designs are those that use channeled foam, giving them sort of a vertical Michelin Man look. The channeled foam flexes and moves with you better than slab-sided, water-skier-type models. The PFD should fit snugly enough so it doesn't ride up around your head when you're in the water, but still allow complete freedom of arm-swinging movement.

Your PFD should have *at least* one pocket, and two or more are better, for carrying emergency signaling equipment and odds and ends. A lash tab for attaching a strobe or knife is a good feature, too. Some of the best PFDs I've seen are British, with three or four pockets on the front plus a huge one on the rear, which can hold a lightweight jacket, survival items, or even an inflatable mini rescue raft for serious expeditions.

PFDs are rated in categories from type I to IV. A type I is designed for offshore yachting use, with at least 22 pounds of flotation and a buoyant collar designed to turn an unconscious person face-up. A type IV is a simple cushion or throw ring. Most paddlers use a type III, which provides plenty of flotation (minimum 15 $\frac{1}{2}$ pounds) and much better freedom of movement than a bulkier type. Fifteen pounds doesn't seem like a lot of buoyancy, but an average human weighs only about 12 pounds in the water.

Since a PFD can interfere with the spray skirt of a kayak, many models intended for sea kayaking either are very short or include a bottom section that can be flipped up to clear the skirt.

As for color, the same goes for PFDs as for boats—the brighter the better, preferably some shade of red or yellow.

SPRAY SKIRT

The spray skirt, which forms a seal between you and the kayak, has to balance several qualities. First, it must be waterproof. It needs to fit tightly enough so that the heaviest wave cannot dislodge it, yet you must be able to yank it off quickly in an emergency. The deck of the skirt—the flat part that stretches around the cockpit rim—must be taut so water doesn't pool on it and leak through, but the

Your PFD should be snug, but allow complete freedom of movment.

chest tube, or chimney, needs to be comfortable and allow free-dom of movement.

The best spray skirts—the ones I've found to combine all these qualities—incorporate a neoprene deck sewn and bonded to a coated-nylon chest tube. All-nylon spray skirts—particularly the cheap ones that don't have a separately constructed chest tube—are prone to sagging in the deck, and all-neoprene skirts, while waterproof and taut, can be very confining around your torso, and hot as well if you're paddling in warm weather.

I'm partial to the excellent spray skirts from Snap Dragon Design in Seattle, but there are other quality brands as well. Make sure the skirt you buy is properly sized for your cockpit opening. If you can't afford the combination neoprene-nylon spray skirts, which cost around $100 to $125, Snap Dragon has an all-nylon skirt with a deck of heavy Cordura, which is less susceptible to sagging than lighter oxford nylon.

The big nylon loop at the front of the spray skirt is the *release loop,* which you grab and yank to remove the skirt in a hurry. Most spray skirts have a certain amount of adjustment in the perimeter elastic; this is where you must experiment to balance tightness with quick removal. An accessory you might consider is called the Kayak Safe. It looks like a big release loop, except it attaches to the underside of the front of your cockpit and extends out the front of the spray skirt. The Kayak Safe will instantly pop off the tightest spray skirt. When you're starting out in kayaking, I suggest leaving the skirt fairly loose so you know you can get it off quickly; you're unlikely to be paddling in breaking waves for a while.

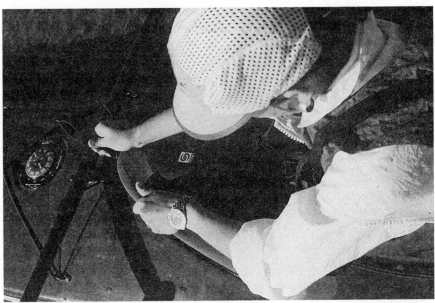

A well-designed spray skirt with a taut deck keeps water from pooling and leaking into your lap.

Other Equipment

PADDLE FLOAT

A paddle float is a device, either inflatable or made from closed-cell foam, designed to be slipped over one of the blades of your paddle. When the other end of the paddle is secured to the kayak, the float acts as an outrigger, drastically increasing the stability of the kayak, and making it possible for a paddler who has capsized and fallen out of the cockpit to climb back in.

As you'll read in chapter 4, the best way to recover from a capsize is with an Eskimo roll. However, even expert rollers can sometimes fail, for any number of reasons, and find themselves treading water next to an upside-down kayak. A paddle float offers an excellent backup system.

I carry an inflatable paddle float because of its compactness; it only takes two or three breaths to inflate, and the air inside holds it very tightly onto the paddle blade; in fact, it's best to slip it over the paddle before you inflate it.

The advantage of the foam floats is that they can't develop leaks. The downside is they are bulkier and must be strapped tightly onto the paddle blade to stay secure. Either type will do the job, though, and one or the other should always be on your kayak.

Other Auxiliary Floats

Recently, several new devices have been introduced whose purpose is to either replace the paddle float or augment it. A couple of these might be useful in certain situations; others are at best redundant and at worst might prove a hindrance. One device uses a CO_2 cartridge to inflate a float the size of a fat bed pillow. The deflated pillow is stored on deck; in the event of a capsize, you pull it free with one hand and trigger the CO_2 cartridge. As the pillow inflates, you lean on it to right your kayak.

There are several significant problems with this device. First, it's almost impossible to use without first letting go of the paddle—an extremely bad idea. Second, once you're back upright you have a giant air pillow flapping around in the breeze. After it's deflated you must install a new cartridge before it can be used again as intended. Since the conditions that cause a capsize normally don't go away after just one flip, you're left without anything.

A paddle float can help you get back into the boat in the event of a capsize.

A much more promising product employs a pair of inflatable sponsons that, after being inflated orally, are strapped securely one on each side of the cockpit. It's a much slower arrangement to put together, but very secure once attached. While not a substitute for a paddle float (or an Eskimo roll), it's effective, for example, for assisting a weak, sick, or injured paddler. As such I would consider carrying one on an extended expedition, but not necessarily as standard rescue equipment for day trips.

Other Equipment

BILGE PUMP

Sooner or later, water *will* get into your boat—a rough landing or launching, a bouncy crossing, or just a leaky spray skirt; it'll find a way. Sometimes it's just a few ounces, which can be ignored until you're on shore, then swabbed out with a big sponge. Now and then, however, you might find yourself with 5 or 10 gallons sloshing back and forth between your legs. You'll need something to get it out.

The simplest device is a bailer, such as a half-gallon juice pitcher with a handle. For emptying a swamped cockpit on the beach, nothing is faster. On the water, however, problems arise. First, you have to unsnap the spray skirt from the cockpit rim; even then some cockpit openings are too tight for convenient bailing. And if the weather is rough, you could find more water coming in than you're getting out. You'll do better with a mechanical pump.

The most common bilge pump on this side of the Atlantic is the cylindrical plastic model sold in every sea-kayak store in the country. This pump, which looks and operates like a fat bicycle pump, is inexpensive and very powerful—as long as you can use two hands to operate it. If your boat is beached, it works great. If you're on the water in calm conditions and can park the paddle and take off the spray skirt, it works great. If you're out in rough weather and need one hand to brace with your paddle while you pump with the other, it's not a whole lot better than a bailer. You can stick the pump down the tube of your spray skirt, grip it with your thighs, and pump with one hand, but the effectiveness is greatly reduced. Nevertheless, the cylindrical pump is a good model to start with, since it's cheap and most of your practicing will be in calm conditions. You can consider alternatives later—and keep the old one as a backup.

My favorite bilge pumps are the built-in type, common on British kayaks but curiously scarce in the United States. A built-in pump, while not as fast as a cylindrical pump in ideal conditions, requires only one hand to work, is instantly deployable at any time, and cannot be lost overboard. The lever motion also seems to me to be less tiring than an up-and-down movement.

Fortunately, the Henderson Chimp pump, the most common deck-mounted pump, can be retrofitted to many different models of kayak. It is bolted through the deck right behind the cockpit. I like having it on my weak-hand side so I can hold the paddle and brace with my strong hand.

An interesting alternative to manual pumps is an electric model. The advantage is that you just flip a switch and the pump takes off, emptying the boat while you devote your full attention to other matters. The downside is it's a battery-operated device subject to failure like any other. I've used electric pumps now and then and only once had a problem, when someone inadvertently flipped the switch on the beach and ran the battery down. But all it takes is one such incident at the wrong time. If you decide on an electric pump, I suggest carrying a backup manual pump, too.

Incidentally, double kayaks should have two pumps. It doesn't matter whether they're both built-ins, or one's a built-in and the other a portable, or whatever. The extra volume in a double is often combined with proportionally less flotation in the end compartments than a single would have, making it vital to remove the water as quickly as possible to regain full control.

DRY BAGS AND DRY BOXES

Even the most waterproof cargo compartments will leak. If you carry gear that you don't want wet, it should always be kept in dry bags. The bonus is that packing your gear in dry bags gives you backup flotation in the event of a serious leak, or even a disaster such as the loss of a hatch cover or a blown-out bulkhead. Even heavy items like tents and stoves, which would sink by themselves, will float inside a dry bag thanks to the air trapped with them.

I prefer heavy-duty PVC dry bags; they seem to resist pinhole leaks better than lightweight nylon bags. If a leak does develop, it's easy to find by holding the bag up to the sun and looking inside; then just dab on a drop of seam sealer. The clear bags that allow you to see their contents are great, but inevitably less durable.

If you plan on doing any multiday touring, buy your dry bags in several colors so you can code the contents: food in blue, clothes in red, and so on. The medium sizes seem to work best all around; they're much easier to stuff in nooks and crannies than larger sizes.

Dry boxes are useful for fragile items, or those that might puncture a dry bag. I use a small Pelican Case for my first-aid kit,

Dry bags and boxes keep your gear dry, and provide backup flotation.

and two clear-lidded acrylic boxes from Underwater Kinetics for tools, spare parts, and such. Another good product is the Watersafe, which looks like a glorified Ziploc bag but is much more waterproof (down to 200 feet) and durable, given its nylon exterior case. The Watersafe comes in several sizes, and works great for anything from wallets and car keys up to binoculars.

SIGNALING DEVICES

The chances that you will ever need outside assistance while you're paddling are very slim. However, you should never paddle without at least a couple of ways of attracting outside help, just in case. Even if you never need them for yourself, you might someday need them to assist someone else.

A signal mirror is an incredibly effective way to attract attention on sunny days. Aircraft pilots have reported seeing the flash from a mirror over 25 miles away. A small mirror will fit in the pocket of your PFD; you'll never know it's there until you need it.

Buy a true signal mirror, with a sighting hole through the center. These are vastly easier to aim accurately. Personally, I also prefer a real glass mirror, which will retain its shine for years. Acrylic versions are lighter but must be treated with more care (they usually come with a soft pouch, which helps). Whichever one you decide on, practice annoying your neighbors with it at home so you won't have to stop and read the instructions at an inconvenient time.

The nighttime substitute for a signal mirror is a strobe. A personal strobe is visible from well over a mile away on a clear night, and will flash about once every second for up to eight hours on one or two batteries.

Signaling gear—shown here, a VHF radio, meteor flare, and mirror—will attract attention should you or a companion need assistance.

Personal strobes are available for under $20, but for around $60 you can get the best: the ACR Firefly, which operates off two alkaline AA cells and is very powerful. The strobe should be pinned to your PFD at all times.

Another great way to attract attention is with compact meteor flares. These are about the size of a fat fountain pen and send a little flare shooting about 300 feet into the air. They work extremely well at night, and not too bad on overcast days either. Three of them will fit in a single pocket of your PFD and set you back less than $20.

These three items—mirror, strobe, and flares—are the basis of a solid signaling system. The strobe can be clipped to the lash tab of your PFD, and both flares and mirror will fit into a single pocket. This way you'll always have some means of summoning help, even if you become separated from your kayak. That is, as long as the PFD is on you and not strapped on the rear deck of the boat.

If you plan on doing any multiday tours, you should beef up your basic signaling kit. I'd suggest adding a distress flag, such as the excellent See/Rescue, which is a bright orange, floating polyethylene streamer 6 inches wide and 25 feet in length. It fits in a compact hard case and clips to your deck bungees. Another smart addition is a parachute flare or two, such as the Pains-Wessex. These are expensive—about $40 each—but will make the area around your kayak look like the Normandy landing when you pull the release. They send a brilliant flare nearly 1,000 feet high; it then floats slowly to earth, burning the entire time. Other possibilities include smoke flares, handheld flares, and air horns. The latter are useful if you paddle in areas where sudden fogs might catch you out.

WHISTLES

I've listed whistles separately from signaling devices because even the loudest cannot be relied on to attract outside help; the sound just fades too quickly, especially when it's windy and/or the waves are kicking up—exactly when you might need assistance. Whistles are, however, very good for alerting nearby companions that something is up. All the members of your group should keep a plastic whistle clipped to the zipper pull on their PFDs.

VHF AND OTHER RADIOS

VHF (Very High Frequency) radios are very common for short-range marine communication. Virtually all power- and sailboats carry them, and should (although not all do) continuously monitor the emergency channel, 16, or the hailing channel, 9. VHF radios are also useful for general communication between boats, and can pick up weather broadcasts if you're close enough to a transmitting station.

The limitation of VHF is that it's generally restricted to line-of-sight use. Two kayakers will be over the horizon from each other, and out of range, if separated by a couple of miles. But in areas with a reasonable density of large-boat traffic, a VHF is an excellent means of communication.

In recent years the size (and price) of handheld VHF units has steadily decreased; some are no bigger than a small cell phone. It's smart to spend a little extra for a waterproof model—check the warranty to determine if the unit is really *guaranteed* waterproof. Even so, I keep mine in a clear, waterproof PVC case designed for it.

Another range of frequencies was recently designated for private use by the FCC. Called "Family Radio Service," these radios are designed specifically for intergroup communication, not attracting outside help. But they're just fine for keeping in touch with your companions (up to around 2 miles), and are astonishingly compact. Models such as the Motorola Talkabout sell for less than $150 each.

KNIFE

Buy a high-quality rescue knife—either a folding model such as the Spyderco Delica, or a fixed-blade model such as the Gerber River Runner—and then make a vow *never* to use it for anything but a real emergency. No slicing cheese, no cutting cord to make tent guylines. Use your Swiss Army knife for mundane chores.

Your rescue knife should never be used for incidental tasks.

Keep the rescue knife clipped to your PFD, where it's available instantaneously.

Your chances of ever desperately needing a rescue knife—say, to cut line in which you've become tangled, or to slice clothing off an injured paddler—are slim. But then, so are your chances of needing flares or a signal mirror or your seat belt or fire insurance. It's just dumb to take the risk when prevention is so easy.

MEDICAL KIT

I always carry a comprehensive first-aid kit in my boat. Especially if you decide to take up touring, you will often be far from medical help, so you should be as self-sufficient as possible. I like the marine-type first-aid kits from Adventure Medical Kits and Atwater Carey. They're expensive, but they include nearly everything (except prescription drugs) that you're likely to need on anything short of a major expedition. Both companies offer add-on units for special situations, allowing you to customize the kit to suit your needs.

CLOTHING

One of the most common mistakes made by sea kayakers—beginners as well as those who should know far better—is underdressing for the water conditions. While it's tempting to wear shorts and a T-shirt when the air temperature is 70 degrees F, in many popular paddling areas the water temperature is significantly colder than the air temperature. Weather on the water can also change dramatically in a matter of minutes, turning a calm, sunny outing into a tempestuous struggle. Since water conducts heat away from a human body about *25 times faster than air,* capsize into, say, 45-degree water wearing shorts and a T-shirt and you'll have about 5 to 10 minutes to get back into the kayak before your body, in a futile attempt to maintain its core temperature, shuts down circulation to your extremities, and you become incapable of helping yourself. Within an hour, if no one spots you and gets you out of the water, you'll be dead (assuming you're wearing a PFD; otherwise the end will be much quicker).

That's an awfully morbid scenario to contemplate while exploring an exciting new sport. But it is utterly simple to eliminate the possibility of such a predicament. Just dress with the *expectation* that you'll wind up in the water. Thanks to the wide range of materials available to the sea kayaker today, it's usually easy to choose outerwear that will be comfortable to paddle in yet offer adequate protection in the event of a capsize.

A lot of kayaking books offer charts listing survival time in different water temperatures. I eschew doing so, simply because of the immense number of variables involved in such a situation: currents and sea state; your age, condition, and body type; even the length of time since you last ate. Suffice to say that the U.S. Coast Guard considers hypothermia a danger in any water under 70 degrees F.

The minimum defense against hypothermia, in water that's merely chilly, is a layer of synthetic underwear beneath a waterproof outer layer, such as a coated-nylon or Gore-Tex jacket and pants. In the event of a capsize and wet exit, the underwear will hold a layer of water next to your skin, where it can be warmed by your body heat; the outer layer will help slow the circulation of exterior, colder water.

This paddler is well dressed for the cold-water conditions in which she is paddling.

The next step up involves a relatively new, and very versatile, fabric generically known as *thermal stretch fabric*. It comprises an outer layer of Lycra, often impregnated with Teflon for water repellency, backed by an elastic, waterproof-yet-breathable laminate, with an inner layer of synthetic fleece. When immersed the fleece traps a layer of water next to your body, assisted by the close-fitting nature of the elastic outer layer. Yet while you're paddling the fabric breathes well, making thermal stretch fabric a good choice when water temperatures are cold but the air warm. You can buy a farmer john, which covers your legs and torso while leaving your arms free, or a full body-covering suit. With a fleece jacket and a waterproof outer jacket, which can be put on or shed as desired, the comfort range of a thermal stretch outfit is really impressive.

When water temperatures dip into the 50s, it's time to consider a wet suit. This functions similarly to thermal stretch fabric, except the water-trapping qualities of neoprene are greater still, extending your tolerable water-temperature range down into the lower 50s. Wet suits, however, are considerably less versatile as paddling garments, and can feel like Saran Wrap on a hot day. To mitigate this, as with thermal stretch garments, I use a farmer john style when the air is warm, to facilitate evaporative cooling, and a full-coverage style for colder conditions.

If you use a wet suit, be sure to buy one made for kayakers rather than scuba divers. A kayaking wet suit allows greater freedom of movement in the arms for paddling. Wet suits come in a variety of thicknesses; those designed for paddling are generally from 1.5 to 3 millimeters thick, a range that offers a compromise between warmth and freedom of movement.

The ultimate in paddling protection is a dry suit, which, as its name implies, completely seals your legs, torso, and arms from contact with the water. A waterproof material—either coated nylon or nylon with a Gore-Tex membrane—is combined with stretchy latex seals at the wrists, ankles, and neck. You enter the suit through a long, diagonal waterproof zipper in either the front or the back of the suit—a truly claustrophobic experience.

While a dry suit isolates you from the water, it actually does little to insulate you from it. For that you wear a layer of synthetic underwear and, normally, a fleece midlayer. Of course it's vital not to compromise the integrity of the suit—one gash and it's rendered useless. With tough modern fabrics this is unlikely, but you should be aware.

Dry suits are really only suitable for the harshest conditions. Even the Gore-Tex models, which allow some body moisture to escape, become uncomfortable in any but very cool air temperatures.

Your head radiates as much heat as your entire torso if left uncovered. A fleece or wool watch cap offers good insulation and can be pulled down over your ears if desired. Cover it with the

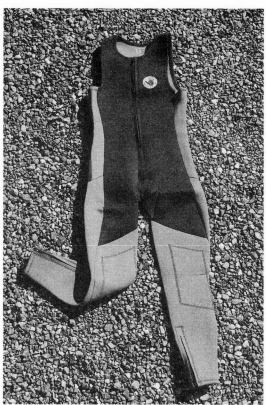

A farmer john wet suit protects while allowing
unrestricted arm movement.

hood on your paddling jacket and you'll gain both warmth and
rain protection. For colder paddling a neoprene wet-suit hood provides serious protection, even in the event of a capsize.

It's essential that you protect your hands from cold as well,
since they're your tools if you get into trouble. Neoprene gloves are
very effective for this, in almost any conditions. As with wet suits,
make sure you buy gloves designed for paddling rather than diving. They'll usually be slightly precurved to help you grip the paddle, and they'll have a nonskid material on the palm. For really
cold conditions you can add *pogies,* which are neoprene coverings
that fit over the paddle shaft and into which you slip your hands.
When using pogies you should always have gloves on, too; in the
event of a rescue situation, you'll have to pull your hands free of
the pogies.

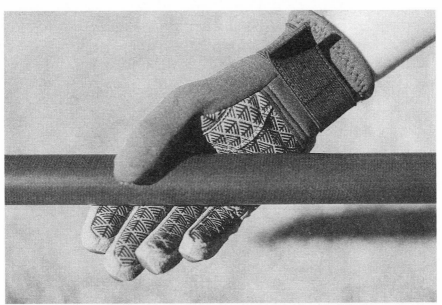
Neoprene gloves are excellent for keeping your hands warm even when wet.

Neoprene will keep your feet warm; however, what with launchings, landings, and the normal dregs of water that tend to collect in the boat, neoprene booties almost always seem to be damp if not actually wet. I like combining booties with a pair of genuine British Wellies, knee-high rubber boots that will keep your feet dry unless you step in water over their tops (in which case they become very effective anchors). With Wellies over neoprene booties I can wade in and out of shallow cold water with impunity, knowing that in an offshore emergency I can kick them free and still retain protection.

In hot climates and warm water, hypothermia is obviously of little concern. However, too much sun exposure can ruin a trip very quickly, not to mention the more insidious danger of skin cancer. Avoid the temptation to wear short-sleeved shirts—holding your arms out to paddle is like putting them on a spit. Choose lightweight cotton or nylon shirts in light colors, and a medium-brimmed hat (rather than a wide one, which will catch the wind annoyingly). I've worn an Ultimate Hat for many years with scarcely any sign of wear. Shorts are fine as long as you keep the spray skirt fastened; otherwise long pants of similar material to the

In hot weather, light-colored clothing and a hat will keep you cool and prevent sun exposure.

shirt are better. Sport sandals are great for footwear, unless you're paddling in very rocky areas and need more protection for your arches and ankles. Then the new breed of amphibious water shoes offer more support and armor.

Don't neglect sunscreen, even if you think you're completely shaded. I once suffered an excruciating sunburn on my septum—that's the little bridge between your nostrils—from sunlight reflecting off the water on a 15-mile crossing. And don't forget good sunglasses, which will prevent serious eye fatigue. I like the double-gradient models from Bausch & Lomb for both desert and Arctic paddling.

ROOF RACKS AND STORING

Even if you're fortunate enough to own a beachfront condo, sooner or later you'll want to explore new territory with your kayak, and that involves transporting it by car. I've seen many people doing so with a couple of towels between boat and roof, and bungees holding the two vehicles together, but that's really tempting fate (a nice way of saying, "That's really stupid"). You should plan on spending about 10 percent of the cost of your new boat on a quality roof rack and saddle system from a company such as Thule or Yakima.

The saddles from either of these companies are excellent, and will safely hold a kayak down through fierce winds and rough roads. Their only downside is that it's difficult for one person to load or unload boats; even two people can have trouble with a tall sport utility vehicle. Yakima has addressed this problem with its Hully-Roller system, a saddle that incorporates soft rollers to allow easy loading from the back of the vehicle. The rollers lock down once the kayak is in place, creating a platform that, while not as stable as a wraparound saddle, is certainly adequate for most situations. The company has recently introduced a kit comprising a rear roller and a front standard saddle, optimizing both loading ease and security.

If you've got room at home, store your kayak up off the floor. Nylon slings hung from the garage rafters are excellent; 2-by-4 brackets bolted to the wall work fine, too, especially if you contour and pad them a bit. Proper support is absolutely vital if you own a rotomolded boat, or the whole kayak can sag. Slings or brackets should be located under the front and rear bulkheads, the stiffest areas of the hull.

Never, under any circumstances, store a plastic boat in the sun—it will die an early death. Some sort of shade is essential. Even a fiberglass boat should be shaded; otherwise the gelcoat will oxidize and the deck rigging will rot. Don't wrap a boat left in the sun

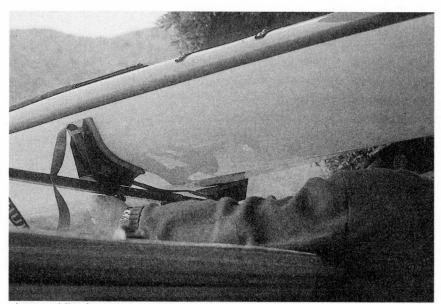

These saddles from Thule grip the kayak's hull securely.

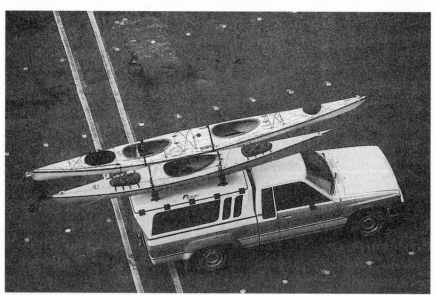

Even big doubles ride safely on a top-quality rack system.

in a plastic tarp in an attempt to protect it; this creates an oven effect that might be worse than direct sun.

In damp climates, kayaks should be stored with the hatch covers off to prevent mold. Where I live (southern Arizona), mold is the least of my worries; I leave the hatch covers closed to keep out scorpions, rattlesnakes, and pregnant coyotes looking for den sites.

PART TWO

TECHNIQUES

Now you've outfitted yourself with high-quality gear, and you know what that means. Yep—no blaming the equipment for what comes next.

If you're learning on your own, I recommend that you read through this entire section first, rather than studying one move and then going right out and trying it. Sea-kayak technique, while easy to assimilate, relies on an integrated series of moves; you should have at least a familiarity with the whole picture before you begin.

CHAPTER 3

BASIC STROKES

Everyone hates looking like a beginner. Well, not everyone—men are more terrified by it than women. That's why we don't ask for directions or read instructions.

With some sports, there's just no way to avoid the amateur look. Ice skating, for example—*everyone* looks goofy their first time on ice skates, which is why men frequently refuse to even try it. However, sea kayaking is an exception to the rule. With careful study of this chapter I can virtually guarantee that, within 15 minutes of your first strokes, you will appear to any and all onlookers to be a perfectly competent paddler. Note that you won't actually *be* competent—that takes practice. But you'll look good and, all kidding aside, will have a solid foundation of technique from which to hone your skills.

First I'm going to offer a narrative account of your introductory paddle. Sit back and read, or sit in your kayak and follow along with some of the movements. After you've read this chapter all the way through, go out on the water and have some fun. Remember to take things at your own pace, trying each new technique when you're ready.

A FIRST PADDLE

You've chosen a sheltered harbor and a calm morning to practice. Lay the kayak at the water's edge, and give it a quick once-over to make sure everything looks okay. (Rudder cables and fittings straight? Rudder raised? Hatch covers secured? Spare paddle in place?). Then sit in the cockpit to confirm the correct rudder-pedal and seat adjustment. Your knees should be comfortably bent rather than straight out in front of you, so that you can brace them on the underside of the deck. Hop out and put on your spray skirt, either by stepping into it or pulling it over your head, then put your PFD over the skirt. Check to make sure your signal mirror and three flares are in the pocket, and your strobe is clipped to the lash tab (yeah, it's eight o'clock in the morning and you'll be home by lunch, but take it anyway).

Since you're wearing sandals and don't feel like getting your feet wet yet, you're going to do a dry launch. Position the kayak so it's pointing straight offshore with the bow and front half in the water and afloat; now you can just step into the cockpit without getting wet. Rest your paddle across the front deck and step into the cockpit, placing your foot right on the centerline in front of the seat so the boat won't rock back and forth. Lift your other foot in,

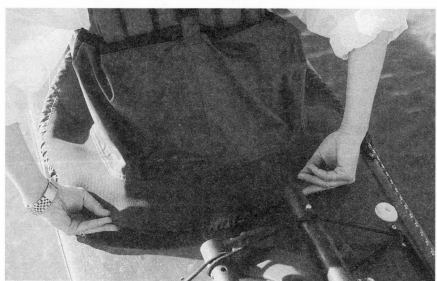

Attach the spray skirt at the rear of the cockpit first.

then lean down and grasp each side of the cockpit rim with your hands, and slide your feet forward while lowering your rear into the seat.

With your feet on the rudder pedals, secure the spray skirt starting at the back. Reach behind you with both hands and hook the elastic perimeter of the skirt over the cockpit rim. Then work forward on both sides at once, stretching the skirt over the rim as you go until you can pop the front of the skirt over the very front of the cockpit. Make sure—then make sure again—that the release loop is free and easily grasped. If you haven't already done so at home, try yanking the release loop straight up to confirm that you can get the skirt off instantly. Don't get annoyed if it pops off with an annoying *bang* while you're fastening it—it happens to all of us.

Okay—you're ready to go. If there's no one to push you off, you can launch in one of two ways. Either use a hand on one side and your paddle on the other, like a staff, to shove off, or leave the paddle secured to the paddle park or balanced across the cockpit and shove off with both hands. The kayak will float in just a few inches of water.

If you don't mind getting your feet wet, you can save some scratches on the hull by getting in with the kayak floating just off-shore. Straddle the cockpit, then lower your rear into the seat. Do *not* try to get in from one side or step into the boat, or you'll capsize and wind up with a faceful of mud. Once you're sitting in the boat, you can lift your feet in and then proceed as above. If your cockpit is too small to allow lifting your legs in after you're seated, you must sit on the rear deck and get your legs in first—an unstable procedure with the boat in the water. Try bracing the paddle across the rear of the cockpit with one blade resting on the sand, as an outrigger. If that's still too insecure, you're better off doing a dry launch.

Once you're afloat, it's time for some forward propulsion. First of all, here's what *not* to do. Beginners tend to grip the paddle too tightly, and hold it up too high in front of their chests, like Robin Hood fending off Little John's stave thrusts. And their strokes are usually short and choppy, creating more splash than propulsion. Hold the paddle just firmly enough to call it firm, with your hands a little farther apart than shoulder width. Paddle strokes for sea kayaking should generally be low, the blade out of the water no more than a couple of feet above the surface, in contrast to the normal whitewater kayaking stroke in which the paddle

Note the relaxed posture and grip—essential for comfortable paddling.

is aggressively angled deep beneath the surface, and the other end arcs over the paddler's head. You want to put all of the blade in the water, but very little of the shaft.

Your stroke should be long and smooth. Plant the blade in the water forward of the cockpit, and draw it well behind you before lifting it out again. Try to make the blade slice smoothly into the water and emerge cleanly, with as little splashing as possible. Water you displace or even lift with the blade is lost propulsion. Don't worry—you won't be perfectly smooth to start with, but it will come with practice. It's surprising how much effect on efficiency just concentrating on splash can have.

Thousands of words have been written about paddling "technique" or "style," a subject to which I pay little or no heed. One (otherwise decent) book I've read described paddling as a "complex cycle of separate components." Jeez. Any four-year-old can watch someone paddle a kayak and then hop in and do it, too. Paddling is a very instinctive movement, and with time you'll develop your own technique, the efficiency of which will be continuously honed with practice. Just keep a few things in mind:

Keep the paddle as low as possible to avoid fatigue and the effects of wind.

- Try to use your whole upper body, instead of sitting rigidly upright and just moving your arms. The more muscle groups you use, the more efficient you'll be and the less overall fatigue you'll experience. If you need more power, bend slightly forward at the waist and twist your torso with each stroke, so that your back and stomach muscles will contribute to the work.
- Try to imagine yourself pushing with your off hand while pulling with the hand that's moving the blade through the water. This helps the paddle describe a nice flat arc through its movement.
- Keep the thumb of your pulling hand and the fingers of your pushing hand fairly loose to minimize grip fatigue.
- Keep the face of the paddle blade vertical in the water, from its entrance all the way through lifting out.
- Relax! The more relaxed you are, the less tired you'll get. A tense body produces tense, jerky paddling. Tension even affects your stability.

The paddle on the left is unfeathered; the one on the right is feathered—note the blades at angles to each other.

Your stroke should be long and smooth.

PADDLE FEATHERING Most paddles are designed so the blades can be feathered—that is, positioned at right angles, or nearly so, to each other. The main advantage to feathering is that the blade that's out of the water during the stroke is parallel to the surface. In this position it catches less wind when the breeze is in front of or behind you. Most sea kayakers feather their paddles.

However . . . this might sound heretical, but the longer I paddle, the less convinced I am that feathering is necessary or even desirable. Here are my arguments:

- First, a feathered paddle requires you to flex your wrist with each stroke to line up the blade properly. This can lead to stress injury, and indeed I've talked to at least a dozen paddlers who had to *un*feather their paddles during an expedition after suffering wrist or elbow pain.

- Also, although a feathered paddle is less susceptible to head- or tailwinds, it is more likely to be caught by crosswinds and flipped up over your head. Since crosswinds are the most difficult to deal with anyway, it would seem to make sense to optimize paddle position for these situations.

- Finally, it is far, far easier to learn with an unfeathered paddle, particularly that vital, instinctive paddle placement necessary for fast bracing.

So—at the very least, there are good arguments for both paddling styles. If you decide to use an unfeathered paddle, I strongly suggest a narrow blade to minimize the spinnaker effect when you're paddling up- or downwind.

Above all, don't concern yourself with the occasional slipup: a splashy stroke, the paddle shaft banging against the side of the boat, and so forth. It will all smooth out.

Up until now you've been paddling (more or less) straight offshore, but sooner or later you're going to bump into a sailboat or something.

As you stroke with the paddle first on one side, then the other, you'll notice the bow of the kayak move slightly back and forth, a movement called yawing. This happens because your propulsion stroke is off to the side of the boat's centerline; when you push on the left side, the boat wants to turn right, and vice versa. The natural progression of this is obvious: If you paddle on only one side of the kayak, it will describe a gentle turn to the opposite side. You can do this now, alternating sides occasionally, and your boat will describe a series of lazy S's.

If your kayak has a rudder you have an additional, very easy and effective means of turning. You can use the rudder to turn while continuing to paddle normally, or combine the rudder with one-side paddling to turn more quickly. Once you've launched and are in water over a foot or so deep, drop the rudder with the release line. You'll immediately feel the "bite" of the rudder through your feet, and can fine-tune even your straight-ahead course with small foot movements. To turn left, just push with your left foot; to turn right, push right. You'll soon develop a feel for how sharp a turn it's possible to accomplish with a rudder. There is a definite limit—if the rudder blade is pushed over too far, it acts more like a brake than a rudder. You can hear this as the water churns around the blade, and the boat slows noticeably instead of just turning.

Speaking of braking, at some point you'll want to stop. Of course, if you simply quit paddling you'll coast to a halt, but if you want faster immobility just paddle backward. Continue paddling backward and you'll find that, yes indeed, kayaks do have a reverse gear in the transmission, allowing you to retreat from any number of hazards: wading grizzly bears, small-boat sailors emptying their Porta Pottis overboard, or large triangular fins slicing through the water ahead of you. You'll also notice that a rudder is *not* designed to work going backward—water pressure will continuously try to slam it over to one side or the other. Best to keep it centered with

A reverse stroke will stop the boat—or back it up, if you wish.

firm foot pressure, or to lift it out of the water if you've some distance to back up.

Regretfully, at some point you'll have to land. The wet-feet landing is essentially the opposite of launching—paddle to the shallows, pop the spray skirt, then lift both feet out of the cockpit and stand up straddling the boat. Then you can swing a leg over and guide the kayak to shore.

The dry landing can be done two ways. The most stylish effect for onlookers involves paddling at top speed straight at the beach. The bow of the boat slides up 8 or 9 feet, leaving the cockpit above the waterline; you step out nonchalantly, adjust your tie, and head for the club. The only danger in this technique (beyond the obvious abuse to the kayak's bow) comes if the beach is just a tiny bit too steep. In this case your bow will wind up perched on the sand, the stern in the water, with the cockpit essentially hanging in thin air. At this point you will instantly capsize, packing one side of your face and an ear canal with wet sand, and completely spoiling your entrance.

A less dramatic, but safer, option is to approach the beach slowly, at a shallow angle, so that when the bow makes contact with the sand the kayak is almost parallel to the beach. You can use your paddle to push on the sea side and swing the stern in to land, grounding the whole boat. Now lay the paddle across the rear deck so the far blade is lying on the beach, and lean on the shaft as you pull yourself out of the cockpit and step ashore. You've just completed your first solo paddle. From here on out, everything else is refinement.

HOW TO FALL OUT OF YOUR KAYAK As I've mentioned before, you might very well paddle your whole life without experiencing an unintentional capsize. On the other hand, to become a truly competent paddler you need to not only push but in fact deliberately exceed the limits of your kayak while practicing braces, rolls, and rescues. The first thing to do is to learn how to gracefully react when you pass the point of no return and your kayak swaps deck for hull. Like jumping off a high dive, once you try it you'll find it's no big deal.

Getting out of an upside-down kayak is called a *wet exit*. Here's how to practice. In a pool, a lake, or a shallow bay or harbor, look for a spot at least 3 feet deep—less than that and you risk a faceful of mud when you go over—but close enough to shore that you can wade or swim to land, pulling the boat. It's a good idea to use a diving mask for practicing; it prevents water up the nose and allows you a better look at what's going on.

To begin with, leave the spray skirt off, but wear your PFD. Paddle to the spot you've chosen, brace your knees under the deck to hold yourself in place, then take a breath and lean to one side until the boat capsizes. You can let go of the paddle for the first run-through. When you're upside down grasp the cockpit rim on either side of you, release your knees, and tuck-roll out of the cockpit and up to the surface, keeping at least one hand on the cockpit rim. You'll come up facing the rear of the boat. When I assist new paddlers with this procedure, their universal comment upon surfacing is, "That's *it?*" There's just nothing to it.

Let's try it again. This time, when you capsize keep your grip on the paddle, holding it parallel to the kayak with one hand. Take a moment while you're inverted to look around. Not so bad, is it? You'll feel the PFD trying to buoy you to the surface. Roll out of the cockpit as before, but this time maintain your grip on the paddle shaft; use the thumb of that hand to grasp the cockpit rim. Now you've kept control of both boat and paddle throughout the procedure, a vital tactic in any open-water capsize situation.

Next time try it with the spray skirt. Fasten the skirt to the cockpit, making sure the release loop is free and yanking the skirt free a couple of times to make sure it does so easily. When you capsize, use one hand to yank the loop forward and up, popping the skirt free. Now roll out as before. I should mention, although I have *never* heard of this occurring, that if for some weird reason the spray skirt ever gets stuck to the cockpit, it's perfectly possible to roll out of the skirt itself, through the chest tube.

The final step in the practice regimen is to leave off the diving mask and get some water up your nose (you'll find that if you exhale slowly though your nostrils while exiting the boat, water incursion is minimized).

Ingrain this procedure in your subconscious so you don't even have to think about it:

- Keep hold of paddle and boat.
- Yank the spray skirt loop up and forward.
- Tuck-roll out of the cockpit.

PROPER TRACKING

When you begin paddling you'll find it difficult to hold a perfect course—the bow continually drifts off the path, and you have to consciously move it back. It's easy to cheat your way out of this using the rudder (or dropping the skeg if your boat is so equipped), but you'll become a better paddler if you practice holding course without external aids.

The key is developing a stroke that applies equal force on both sides of the kayak—difficult because nearly all of us have one arm stronger than the other. But you can balance your stroke with concentration, and in time it will become natural.

Pick a target to aim at, something precise such as a flagpole or mast a fair distance off, and paddle toward it, attempting to keep the bow pointed right at it. Of course it's impossible to keep the bow dead straight; each time you stroke the boat will yaw slightly. What you're aiming for is to keep the target centered within the arc of the yaw. You'll undoubtedly notice the boat tending one way or the other. Try to slightly increase the power of each stroke on the side the boat is leaning, rather than waiting until you're off course and then applying a corrective move. Try it at different speeds. Once you're able to maintain a pretty straight course, try it without watching the target for increasing periods of time, until you can stay pretty straight for several minutes without checking.

TURNING TECHNIQUE

Using the rudder and/or paddling on one side will turn the kayak with enough alacrity to suit many situations—but not all. For maneuvering around rocks and other multiple obstructions, handling the kayak in rough weather, or paddling with a group, you'll want more precise control.

You've already discovered that when you use the paddle on one side of the boat, the boat turns the opposite way. You can augment this natural tendency by using what's called a *sweep stroke*—a long, arcing stroke that you begin by planting your paddle blade in the water far forward and very close to the hull; in fact the blade is almost pointing the same direction as the bow at the start. You sweep the blade out and back, leaning slightly toward it so the arc extends far from the centerline of the hull, and continue sweeping until the blade winds up almost straight behind you, again almost parallel to the hull. What this sequence does is this:

- As you begin the sweep, the paddle is actually *pushing* the bow in the direction of the turn.
- As the paddle arcs out to the side, it acts like an exaggerated normal turn stroke.
- As the paddle is drawn forcefully back toward the stern, it *pulls* the stern toward it, furthering the turning process.

A powerfully rendered sweep can change your heading by 30 degrees or more, allowing very quick boat placement. It requires no shifting of your grip on the paddle shaft; you simply move both arms farther out to whichever side you're sweeping. (Obviously, you must be careful not to lean too far out when you sweep the paddle; see Bracing, below, for a trick to apply here.)

One advantage to the sweep stroke is that it works even if the boat is sitting still. You can also do a *reverse sweep,* starting at the stern of the boat and ending near the bow, which will turn the kayak the opposite direction of a front sweep.

Your paddle can also be used as an auxiliary rudder. For example, if you want to turn right, trail the paddle blade in the water behind you on your right side. Unlike the sweep stroke, this technique works only if the boat is moving, but it is an old tool—in fact the first rudders were nothing more than oars trailed off ships' sterns this way.

Another way to increase turning power exploits the design of the kayak hull itself.

A kayak that's sitting straight upright usually wants to go straight ahead. It will turn more quickly if you tilt it over on its side—and this rocking technique is one of the fundamental skills practiced by advanced paddlers.

The idea is to use your hips to rock the boat while your body stays vertical—imagine the movements of a hula dancer and you'll get the picture. Done this way, *you* remain perfectly stable—only your boat tilts. What happens is that as you tilt the boat sideways, you're pushing its buoyant center part down into the water, which lifts the bow and stern slightly out of the water—thus shortening the waterline length (remember chapter 1?) and causing the boat

The sweep stroke gets the paddle blade farther out from the boat, and increases turning power.

to turn more quickly. Combining a sweep stroke with this tilt will turn almost any kayak quite handily.

Your instinct will tell you to lean the kayak in the direction of the turn, as if you were riding a bicycle. Ironically, however, the design of most kayaks means they will turn better if leaned in the direction *opposite* the turn. Leaning the boat either way will help, though.

BRACING

Many people consider bracing an advanced technique, but it's one of the first skills I teach new paddlers. Knowing how to brace will increase your confidence level immensely, because it makes you nearly immune to the capsizes that all beginners fear.

Bracing relies on a very simple law of physics. If you sit in your kayak, place one paddle blade flat on the surface of the water, and push down, you and the kayak will tilt the other way. Push down hard enough and you can actually capsize yourself.

The low brace or planing brace will right a kayak that is on the edge of capsizing.

The corollary to this is: If you lean the boat and yourself *toward* the paddle blade and then push down, the action will right you and the boat. In fact, a powerful brace will easily right a kayak that's on the verge of capsizing.

The brace sea kayakers use about 90 percent of the time is called a *low brace,* because it's done from the normal paddling position, with your arms held low. The paddle blade is pushed hard and quickly against the surface of the water, resulting in a strong push in the other direction—enough to counter an unanticipated tilt or gust of wind. The action must be done quickly, because you don't want the blade to sink beneath the surface; if that happens the resistance to being pulled out will tilt you back over toward the paddle. One way to avoid this is to push the blade across the surface in a short, sharp arc as you lean on it, so the blade planes across the water. If you do perform a brace and find that the blade has sunk too far, turn it 90 degrees so you can withdraw it edgewise.

Practice bracing where you practice your wet exits. Experiment with leaning over until you feel the boat begin to capsize, then bracing quickly and firmly. You'll find you can practically put your face in the water and still recover. Use body English to help the brace; for example, if you lean to the right and brace to straighten up, use your hips and your right knee under the deck to help flick the boat level. You'll use this same movement when you learn to roll in the next chapter.

Modifying the basic brace can result in support for several seconds or, indeed, a nearly indefinite amount of time.

If the boat is moving forward when you brace and you tilt the blade slightly up from horizontal, it will plane across the surface as the boat moves, resulting in continuous support as long as the boat coasts. Similarly, if the boat is sitting still and you move the blade across the surface as you brace, the support will be extended for up to several seconds. But you can go far beyond this.

Remember the sweep stroke for turning, and my caution not to lean too far? If you perform a sweep but turn the paddle so it planes on the surface, you'll find that you can lean right out on the paddle, past the point where you would normally capsize. In fact any paddle stroke can be turned into a brace—called a *planing brace*—instantly by turning the blade so it provides support as well as propulsion. One of the most common times to find yourself unstable is when everything seems normal and you're just paddling along, perhaps in a slightly bouncy sea or through a stiff breeze. You're not paying perfect attention when suddenly there's that *whoops!* feeling of being just a tad too far leaned over. Converting your stroke to a brace is instant and, with very little practice, completely instinctive. In time you won't even notice those little whoopses.

The ultimate permutation of the planing brace is called a *sculling brace*. Start with a planing brace but then reverse the direction and tilt of the paddle, then reverse it again, so you wind up stroking a figure-eight on the surface with the blade planing in each direction. Done properly a sculling brace will support a kayak laid completely on its side, with your cheek in the water, for as long as you like. A quick push straight down will then right the boat.

THE DRAW STROKE

Have you ever contemplated parallel parking in a really tight spot and wished you could move your car sideways? In a kayak you *can* move sideways, using something called a *draw stroke.*

A sculling draw stroke will move the kayak sideways through the water.

If you reach out to the side of the kayak and plant the paddle blade in the water with the shaft vertical and the power face of the blade toward you, then pull, the kayak will move toward the paddle. (Don't reach out too far, or you'll capsize!) You can repeat the sequence to move sideways as far as you like, either by lifting the blade from the water and replanting it when you've pulled it all the way to you, or by twisting it 90 degrees and slicing it away from you still submerged.

The ultimate technique for parallel-parking a kayak is a *sculling draw stroke,* which exploits the same figure-eight movement as the sculling brace. This time, however, the blade of the paddle is vertical as you move it back and forth, and the kayak slowly moves sideways.

CHAPTER 4

RECOVERIES AND RESCUES

Sometimes I wish we sea kayakers had picked other terms to describe the contents of this chapter. *Recoveries* and *rescues* make it sound as though something desperate has happened when all that has occurred is that you've tipped over. With a modicum of training and practice in the proper procedures, such an event need be nothing more than a hiccup in the day in about 99 percent of circumstances. In fact, *deliberately* capsizing and then rolling back up is useful in many situations—cooling off on a hot day, looking around underwater with a diving mask, avoiding low-flying aircraft. . . .

So the first step in dealing with a possible capsize is to get over the idea that it's some sort of disaster. You've already seen how easy it is to exit an overturned kayak. Now I'm going to cover a half-dozen ways to get back in, or to avoid having to get out in the first place.

This chapter is about contingencies. It might be a long time before you tackle the kind of open-water conditions conducive to an unintentional capsize. But it's never too early to learn the proper techniques. The more you know, the more self-confidence you'll have—confidence that will let you enjoy challenging routes and conditions you'd have to avoid otherwise. And practicing rescues with friends in controlled conditions is a lot of fun.

First, a couple of definitions. A *recovery* means that after a capsize you right yourself by means of an Eskimo roll, and no other tactics are needed—you simply continue on. A *rescue* is necessary when, for whatever reason, you have to wet-exit the boat and must right your upside-down craft and get back in. This can occasionally happen to even an expert roller, for any number of reasons. A rescue can be accomplished without outside assistance—say, for example, by using a paddle float—in which case it is called a self-rescue; if done with the aid of another paddler it's called an assisted rescue.

RECOVERY AND RESCUE OPTIONS

Kayakers usually capsize in one of two basic scenarios. The first is when they're not paying attention in only moderately bouncy conditions, and a wave or gust of wind catches them off guard—*sploosh.* The second occurs when they happen to be caught out in truly bad weather, and the boat is knocked over despite their efforts. In either case, the following methods of regaining control follow a distinct order of preference:

- Rolling back up. This is the best option, both because it's the fastest and because you never leave the cockpit or remove the spray skirt; very little water gets in, and you don't get completely soaked. A roll can take less than five seconds to accomplish, after which you simply continue on your way. Last, but not least, rolling is by far the most stylish option.
- Reentry and roll. If, for some reason, you fail to roll and have to wet-exit, you can reenter the cockpit of your inverted kayak and roll back up. This is also very quick, and doesn't require the assistance of other paddlers. It allows you to pick the best window in conditions to initiate the roll (as well as take a big breath). It does, however, result in considerably more water in the cockpit, which must be pumped out, and thoroughly soaks you.
- Reentry and roll with a paddle float. This is one of my favorite backup strategies. Using a paddle float almost guarantees a successful roll and gets you back in the boat without outside

help even in rough conditions. In addition, you can brace with the paddle and float while pumping out the cockpit.

- Paddle float rescue. Righting the kayak from the water, then using the paddle float as an outrigger while climbing back into the cockpit is a controversial technique, but if done properly it can be useful, even in rough conditions.
- Assisted reentry. If another paddler is available to help, and conditions aren't so bad that he or she is fully occupied otherwise, an assisted reentry is very easy to accomplish in many situations.

The redundancy afforded by these options means that the paddler familiar with all of them can recover from a capsize in virtually any conditions short of a full hurricane.

THE ESKIMO ROLL

The Eskimo roll is viewed by new paddlers with the same awe given to a magician's trick. Yet with competent instruction, almost anyone can learn to roll in an afternoon. Can you learn from a book? Absolutely—though having an experienced observer nearby will help you speed up the process. I suggest reading, then taking a one-day class, then practicing by yourself or with friends. Still, in the text below I'm going to assume you're on your own.

Although you'll see articles and books that show a staggering variety of rolls, I recommend learning just two: the *Pawlata roll*— taught slightly differently as the pivot roll—and the *screw roll*, which is in some ways a progression of the Pawlata. These two will cover you in any situation you're likely to encounter. If, for the sake of variety or historical interest, you go on to try other types of rolls, great. But the screw and Pawlata rolls are all you need.

The Pawlata roll is the simplest. It is, in essence, a powerful low brace—except you're doing it from *under water*. It requires you to shift your grip on the paddle to extend it; in fact you wind up with one hand holding the end of the near blade, and the other about halfway down the shaft. You reach up to the surface with the paddle held out to the side of the kayak and, with the blade flat on the surface, give a sharp downward push.

The screw roll is similar, except it's usually not necessary to shift your grip on the paddle from your normal position (although you can if you need more leverage). The screw roll uses the lift of a planing brace to right the boat—imagine a sweep stroke that you've converted to a brace, except, again, accomplished from under water.

The key to any roll—the "crux move" in climbers' terms—is something called the *hip flick*. There comes a point during the roll when the buoyancy of your PFD plus the lift of the paddle have brought your head to the surface. Instinct is screaming at you to keep lifting your head and body from the water. But the kayak is still in a stable, upside-down position, and the proper sequence involves righting the kayak first, with a sharp "flick" of your hips. Once the kayak rotates beyond a certain point it will continue trying to pop upright instead of back over, and that's when you can use the last push or sweep of the paddle to lift your torso clear.

It's worthwhile to schedule a practice session in your kayak, either in a pool or next to a low dock, to do nothing but practice hip flicks (you can also hold the hand of a friend standing in the water next to you). With your spray skirt on to avoid getting too much water in the cockpit, hold on to the pool edge with one or both hands and lean toward that side, putting your head and torso down in the water until you feel the kayak pass its stable phase and start to capsize. Then, keeping your head down, use a quick jerk of your hips to rotate the kayak back upright. Your hands should not do any of the work except for holding up your torso; in fact you'll notice that most of the weight is taken off them when you flick the boat upright. Repeat the exercise until you become familiar with the motion.

The Paddle Float Roll

The next step is to try an actual roll, using a paddle float. Let's go back to the shallow bay where you practiced wet exits and braces.

Paddle out to your practice area and install the paddle float on the left blade of your paddle (you're free to reverse all the following instructions if you choose, and roll up on the right instead). You can leave the spray skirt off if you like, but it will help keep water out of the cockpit. Wear your PFD and a diving mask. Make sure you're well braced in the cockpit—believe it or not, your biggest trouble throughout the following procedure will be staying inside the boat. Hold the paddle parallel to the kayak on your right side, with the float forward. Take a breath, capsize on your left, and wait until the kayak comes to rest inverted. Now you're going to reach up to your right—which would be to the *left* of the upside-down kayak if you were looking at it from the surface—extending your left arm across your body to reach the paddle float out to the side of the kayak. Your right arm will be bent, and the right paddle blade should be in the air over the upturned hull. Paddle and kayak form a T. Pull down with your left hand, which will begin rotating the boat and raising your head to the surface, where you can take a breath. Now, with the kayak roughly sideways in the water, simultaneously flick the boat upright with a strong jerk of your hips and push down firmly on the paddle, lifting your torso and head clear of the water. The kayak should snap back to a stable position, and you can use a final push on the paddle to sit upright. You've just completed a self-rescue.

The Pawlata Roll

Once you're able to execute the paddle float roll reliably, it's time to convert to a real Pawlata roll. You can do this gradually. First, try a paddle float roll, but while you're upside down shift your grip on the paddle so that your right hand is gripping the end of the right paddle blade, and your left hand is about halfway down the shaft. The power face of the blades should be down. Hold on tightly, because the paddle often tries to pivot in your grip (if you're using a feathered paddle the near blade will be vertical; it won't matter which way it's facing, as long as the power face of the other blade is down).

You'll feel how much more leverage is available in this extended position. Next, start gradually releasing air from the paddle float so that with each successive roll you rely less on the buoyancy of the float and more on the resistance of the blade itself. The key will be developing enough speed in the roll sequence that the paddle blade doesn't sink too far. Continue lowering the air pressure in the float until it's completely flat, then remove it altogether. Note that even the flaccid float adds to the surface area of the paddle blade, so it's a jump from flat float to bare blade. Also, if you own a fat-bladed paddle and a narrow model, you'll have an easier

The Pawlata roll.

time learning with the wide blade, which offers more surface area and support. This roll is perfectly possible with a narrow blade, too, but it takes more power and speed to accomplish it cleanly.

Since there's no way to prevent the blade from sinking a bit during the Pawlata roll, take care getting it out of the water. You can turn the blade at right angles and slice it straight up, but I usually yank it straight out toward me. The friend who taught me the Pawlata, mindful of my heritage, said, "Pretend you're a Viking who's just skewered a Celtic monk, and you need your spear back."

The Screw Roll

Once you've mastered the Pawlata roll, it's time to move up to the screw roll. I say *up* because the screw roll has a couple of advantages over the Pawlata. It's faster, because you don't have to shift your grip on the paddle. It's also more powerful, because you're using the lift of a planing blade instead of simple resistance to it being pushed down through the water. Yet the screw roll, properly done, takes *less* strength than the Pawlata. If you find that you simply cannot develop the strength needed for the Pawlata, the screw roll will almost certainly work for you. Finally, the screw roll has a built-in backup feature: Because the positioning and movements are very close to those you use when performing a sculling brace, if for some reason you fail on your first roll attempt, you can convert to a sculling brace to lift your head to the surface for a breath of air, then quickly reposition the blade and try the roll again.

It's okay to begin practicing the screw roll with a paddle float to get the movements honed, but lowering the air pressure does little good because the float starts to flop around; even when full it prevents the blade from planing the way it should. Better to just chuck it and start clean.

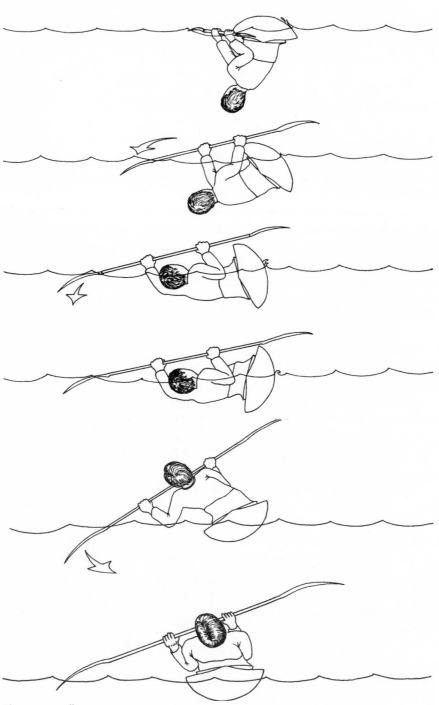

The screw roll.

Set up for the screw roll in the same way you did for the Pawlata, but don't shift your grip on the paddle. From an inverted position lean far forward and toward the surface. Place the forward blade on the surface as close to the bow as possible. Sweep the blade out and back, planing it across the surface and using the lift to raise your head and rotate the kayak. When the paddle is out perpendicular to the boat, your head should be at the surface and the kayak sideways in the water. Now is the time to use a hip flick to right the boat; however, to gain support for this, continue sweeping the blade back around toward the stern instead of pushing down. Lean your torso back with the blade as it sweeps, until you can lift your head and body clear and upright. At the end of the roll you should be leaning back over the rear deck; the paddle blade will be near the stern, and still on or near the surface.

If you have trouble getting enough leverage to complete the roll, go ahead and shift your grip on the paddle, but not as far out as with the Pawlata. Your near hand should grip the shaft just above the blade, with your other hand about halfway out on the shaft.

As with the Pawlata roll, the key to the screw roll is a decisive execution and a powerful hip flick.

REENTRY AND ROLL

Occasionally, even a paddler with a near-perfect Eskimo roll will wind up having to wet-exit. Every now and then a capsize will catch you so unaware that your brain just gets discombobulated, and the next thing you know you're treading water beside an upside-down kayak. The quickest way to regain control is with a reentry and roll. The good thing about this tactic is that it allows you to pick the best window in conditions—a lull in wave sets, for example, if the weather is rough.

If you find yourself in the water after a capsize, remember to hang on to both paddle and kayak—*especially* kayak, since if conditions are rough it can easily be blown away from you faster than you can swim. If worst comes to worst and you lose the paddle, you at least have a spare with the boat. Most books tell you to stay on the downwind side of the kayak to help prevent losing it; however, I've found that the kayak tends to pivot around the paddler, who's acting as a sea anchor, and so winds up on the downwind side anyway. Also, in steep seas an upwind kayak will be constantly trying to run you down. One more thing—if you reenter the boat from the upwind side and time your roll correctly, the wind and waves will actually help you back upright instead of fighting you. So the important thing is to keep hold of the boat, no matter which side of it you're on.

The reentry is essentially a wet exit done in reverse. Position yourself next to the cockpit, facing the stern. Reach under the boat and grab the cockpit coaming, keeping the paddle controlled with one hand. Take a breath and tuck-roll up into the cockpit. Quickly brace your knees under the deck to lock yourself in, then roll up.

This technique does scoop a fair amount of water into the cockpit, which you'll need to pump out as soon as possible. If a companion is nearby, he or she can raft up with you to help steady your boat while you pump or bail. Otherwise consider using a sea anchor or paddle float to help steady yourself.

The reentry and roll can also be done using a paddle float. In fact, if you know how to roll but lack proficiency in rough conditions, I think this is a virtually bombproof self-rescue technique.

THE PADDLE FLOAT RESCUE

The paddle float rescue is maligned by many paddling experts, including a few who, I suspect, have never tried it. They claim it's suitable only for the calmest of conditions, and apparently think that anyone who cannot perform an Eskimo roll in hurricane conditions shouldn't be kayaking.

The truth is, the paddle float rescue can be used in very rough conditions with the proper technique, especially if a sea anchor is employed as well to steady the boat. This rescue has the added advantage of providing a way to steady the kayak after you're back in the cockpit and pumping out the boat.

The critics are right about at least one thing, however—the paddle float is too often viewed as a surefire get-out-of-jail-free card, tucked under the deck bungees and then forgotten by people who never even inflate the thing until they capsize 5 miles offshore in a 40-knot breeze. Like any other recovery or rescue technique, the paddle float rescue is only as effective as the practitioner. If you carry a paddle float (and I think every paddler should), practice using it in as many conditions as possible.

THE SEA ANCHOR If you plan to do much open-water paddling, consider carrying a sea anchor (also called a *drogue*), one of the most useful and least-appreciated accessories you can own.

A sea anchor is nothing but a small parachute designed to be deployed in the water rather than air. A hole in the canopy allows some water to pass through, which helps keep the canopy taut. A long line connects the drogue to the kayak, to allow some elasticity in the system. A drogue will keep the kayak's nose pointed into wind and waves, where it more easily rides over the seas, and will also slow its downwind drift to near nothing.

A drogue is useful during long upwind paddles, when you want a break but don't want to lose ground. It's also very useful during rescues, since it keeps the boat pointed in an optimum direction.

The best sea anchor I've seen for kayaks (in fact it's the *only* one I've seen designed specifically for kayaks) is the Driftstopper, by Boulter of Earth. See appendix 2 for more information.

Here's how a paddle float rescue is accomplished: First, get the capsized kayak back upright. You can sometimes do this simply by heaving up on the near-side cockpit rim, flipping the boat away from you; at other times, however (especially if the boat is loaded with gear), you'll have to scramble over the hull and grab the opposite cockpit rim, then pull the boat back over toward you. This is virtually foolproof, but it does get more water in the cockpit because your weight is forcing it lower.

If conditions aren't too rough, control the kayak with one elbow hooked over the cockpit rim while you inflate the paddle float. With most models it's best to put a single breath in to stiffen it some, then slip it over the paddle blade and finish inflating. The air pressure holds it quite well. If you have a foam paddle float, you

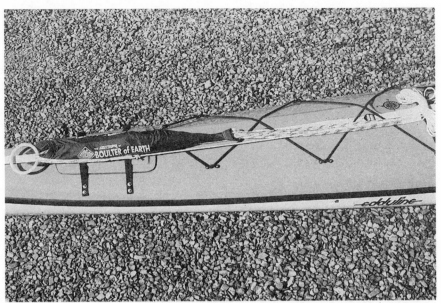

A sea anchor is very useful to prevent the kayak from drifting downwind.

just need to secure the straps over the paddle blade. Fasten the other blade of the paddle across the rear deck of the boat, just behind the cockpit, using whatever rigging you have there— bungees are better than nothing (just), but straps are a big improvement. The more rigid the outrigger arrangement is, the better.

Now you're ready to climb back in. You can get in from either in front of or behind the paddle shaft. I think it's easier to get in from in front unless you have a very small cockpit opening (as on some British boats); then the from-behind approach is better.

Let's assume you've positioned the paddle so it extends from the left side of the kayak. Position yourself next to the cockpit in front of the paddle shaft, which you grip with your right hand. Grab the opposite side of the cockpit rim with your left, then, using a powerful scissors kick, heave your upper body up and over the cockpit onto the rear deck. Be careful not to get too exuberant or you'll fall off the other side of the boat. Don't laugh; I've watched it happen.

Facedown on the rear deck, keep pushing down on the paddle shaft with your right hand, for stability. Lift your legs into the

Reentry using a paddle float.

(a)

(b)

(c)

(d)

(e)

cockpit, then slide down into it until you can twist around and drop your rear into the seat. At all times, keep your center of gravity as low as possible. Once you're seated, fasten the spray skirt to keep waves from dumping more water inside, then lean on the paddle shaft for stability while you pump out the boat.

If the seas are very high when the capsize occurs, you can maintain much better control over the entire procedure by deploying a sea anchor before you inflate the paddle float. You must be ready for the elastic jerk as the drogue catches, but the boat will then be held into the waves and wind. The only downside to using a drogue is that, with the boat held essentially motionless instead of drifting with the weather, the passing seas can seem bigger and faster. However, the advantage of having the bow held upwind solves far more problems than it creates.

ASSISTED RESCUES

If you're paddling with one or more companions, an assisted rescue can be a quick and easy operation—as long as the conditions aren't so bad that your friends are fully engaged in their own struggles to stay upright. Even then, two or three kayaks rafted together —that is, with the paddlers holding on to each other's cockpits— form an astonishingly stable platform.

Side-by-Side Rescue

The simplest assisted rescue requires only one other paddler. Let's say that Dick has capsized and Jane is paddling to assist him. If possible, Dick rights his kayak while Jane paddles over. When she arrives, she positions her kayak next to Dick's so that she can hold on to his cockpit rim. It's easier if she points her kayak the opposite direction to his—so she can hold the front of the cockpit while he climbs in over the rear deck—but not vital. Jane takes Dick's paddle and tucks it under her front deck bungees with her own. Once she has a firm grip on the cockpit rim of Dick's boat, he uses a scissors kick to get out of the water and facedown on the rear deck, in the same position as during a paddle float rescue. He then slides his legs into the cockpit and drops his rear into the seat. At this point Jane can continue to steady his boat while he fastens his spray skirt and pumps the cockpit dry. This procedure works well because the assisting paddler can compensate for the movements of the paddler in the water, keeping the empty kayak level.

If third paddler is handy, he or she can raft up on the opposite side of Jane's kayak and steady her boat, so Jane can pay more attention to helping Dick.

A side-by-side assisted rescue.

An alternative placement of the boats is useful if Dick is too weak to get back in the cockpit from the side. The two assisting paddlers position their boats on either side of the empty one. Dick scoots between his own boat and one of the rescuer's, with an arm over each, and lifts his legs up and over the deck into the cockpit. This procedure is awkward, but takes less strength. I don't like it much if the boats are loaded with gear, because the extra mass in the kayaks tends to crunch the rescuee between them as he or she attempts to scramble back in.

ALL-IN RESCUES

The conditions that cause one capsize very frequently cause several—especially as companions who stop to help or simply gawk forget to watch their own situations. However, it's perfectly possible for two or more capsized paddlers to help each other back into their boats. Each paddler rights his or her boat, then pushes them together bow to stern. One paddler gets between the cockpits and hangs on to both while the second paddler climbs back in from the outside. That second paddler then steadies the other boat for a normal assisted rescue.

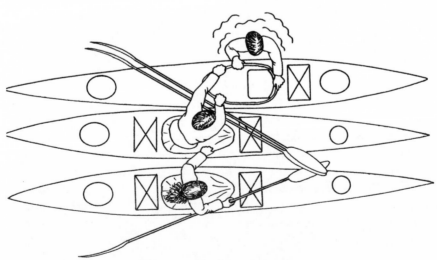

An assisted rescue using a third paddler for extra support.

DOUBLE KAYAK RESCUES

Capsizes of double kayaks are even less common than of singles; nevertheless it can happen, and when it does you're of course left with two paddlers in the water, and one boat. The solution is simple: The two position themselves on either side of the rear cockpit, and one paddler climbs back in. It's best to start at the rear, since this is where the rudder controls are usually located; the first paddler back in can thus begin to control the boat. The rear paddler, by leaning and bracing to the opposite side, can counterbalance the boat while the front paddler climbs in.

TOWING

Occasionally, a situation will arise when you need to tow another boat. It might be because a companion has become sick or injured, or because someone has capsized too near a rough *lee shore* (one toward which the wind is blowing). You can rig a tow line from almost any piece of stout cord. It should be at least 20 feet long; 30 or 40 is better, to allow some elasticity between the two boats. The line can run through the bow loop of the towed boat and fasten to the paddle-park cleats in front of the cockpit, so the towee can cast off (or cut the line) if necessary. The towing kayak should have the line fastened, if possible, behind the cockpit, to maintain the best directional stability—but few boats have the means for this. Tying the line *around* the cockpit rim works well, however, and running it just ahead of the cockpit to a cleat isn't too bad.

The best tow systems I've seen are those sold by Great River Outfitters; these include a jam cleat that attaches behind the cockpit, plus 45 feet of floating line with a snap and an elastic section to absorb shock. It you plan on touring with groups of friends, the investment would be worth it.

The simplest tow arrangement is one boat towing another. You can add a second tow for extra power; if you do, it's best to have the second boat pull the primary towing boat, to keep the forces in line.

If you're towing an injured or sick paddler, consider using inflatable sponsons (chapter 2, page 43) to help steady the kayak.

AFTER THE RESCUE

Once a capsized paddler—whether you or a companion—is back in the kayak, make sure he or she is not suffering from hypothermia or disorientation before continuing. If so, head for shore immediately to dry out. A thermos of hot chocolate or tea is a good restorative, and a dry fleece jacket and/or cap helps, too.

FAILED RESCUES

If you've practiced the above techniques thoroughly, it's extremely unlikely that you'll ever capsize and not be able to regain the cockpit. However, it is a possibility, and you should know what to do.

First, *stay with the boat*. The exceptions to this axiom are few: if you're in immediate danger of being swept out to the open sea and there is land *very* close by, for example, or if you're in the wilderness with no possibility of rescue by another craft, and have no option but to get to shore on your own. Incidentally, it's always smart to have your name and address permanently affixed somewhere in your kayak, as well as a copy of your current itinerary with the dates. That way if your boat is found drifting by itself, the Coast Guard will have some idea of which direction to start searching for you. But in normal paddling circumstances, when you'll be using a radio or signaling device to attract another craft, the kayak makes a far better target for rescuers to find than your head poking 15 inches out of the water. Make every possible attempt to stay with it.

The first thing to do, if you have a VHF radio, is try the emergency channel to summon help from a monitoring boat—or to at least have the crew pass along your SOS to a Coast Guard station. If you get no answer, look for other boats or shore installations within visual range. In daylight deploy your See/Rescue banner if you have one, then use your signaling mirror to flash at the target. At night you should first pop the switch on your strobe to get it blinking, then try a meteor flare by aiming it in a high arc over or in the direction of the target. Don't be tempted to immediately fire off all your flares unless you have a target that you feel can't fail to see you—and even then, use caution. Continue to try the emergency channel on the radio; other boats can shift in and out of range quickly.

CHAPTER 5

ADVANCED OPEN-WATER TECHNIQUES

I know many sea kayakers who have quite happily never ventured beyond lakes or sheltered sea coves in their boats. And that's great—the beauty of the sea kayak is that it can be anything you want it to be, whether a vehicle for quiet contemplation and bird-watching or an ends-of-the-earth expedition machine.

I'll warn you, however—for most people, those gentle paddles around the bay merely whet the appetite. Very soon the horizon calls and you begin to wonder: What's beyond that point? How far it is to that island? What would it be like to paddle around an iceberg?

To challenge open-water conditions in a kayak, you need to become a student of true *seamanship*—a broad and ancient discipline that encompasses knowledge of weather, wind, waves, and currents, and the actions of a craft subject to their whims. Certainly a sea kayak is vastly different than a 60-foot ketch—or a 600-foot cargo ship—but many of the principles are the same.

In this chapter I'll describe many conditions in which, as you read, you might think you would never voluntarily put yourself. However, it is the nature of open-water paddling, with its exposed stretches and long crossings, that sometimes you find yourself forced to continue when less-than-optimum circumstances arise suddenly. The important thing to keep in mind is the astounding seaworthiness of any sea kayak piloted by a capable paddler.

How to put this seaworthiness into perspective? Imagine a lightbulb tossed into the sea. Although fragile if dropped on the kitchen floor, that bulb could ride out the worst storms on the planet with impunity, simply rolling with the forces like a reed bent in the wind. An empty sea kayak, its cockpit sealed shut, would do much the same. It might get rolled and tossed, but its hard shell wouldn't collapse as the proportionally much more fragile hull of a large ship might. Add the paddler, whose skills compensate for the instability caused by his or her extra weight, and you've forged an astonishingly capable team. I'm not suggesting you go try to paddle through weather systems that have been granted human names, but realize that with practice, you can safely negotiate much rougher conditions than you think. And it's an absolute blast to practice with friends in an enclosed and safe harbor or bay, with an onshore wind whipping up whitecaps. You can push your limits as far as you like, knowing that the worst consequence will be a swim to shore. Play sessions like these are the best way I know to build rough-water skills.

MOVEMENTS OF THE SEA—WIND, WAVES, AND CURRENTS

Wind is caused by a number of atmospheric and geographic conditions—low- or high-pressure systems, differential cooling of land and water, Hadley cells, and others. Wind, in its turn, is the ultimate creator of all waves except those produced by boats (wakes), seismic events (tsunamis), and tides (true tidal waves). Sea kayakers rarely have to deal with the latter two, although the former are annoyingly common at times.

Wind-generated waves begin as small ripples, just like those on a pond when a breeze springs up. If the ripples begin at sea and the wind continues, the ripples build in size and combine to form small swells. These build upon themselves to produce large swells, which can travel hundreds of miles across the open ocean before encountering land. The distance over which a wave travels as it builds is called the *fetch;* the longer the fetch, the bigger the wave can grow (given a constant wind speed). In the southern oceans above Antarctica, waves can literally travel unimpeded all the way around the earth, which is why the seas there are noted for their ferocity—storm waves 75 feet high are not uncommon. The height of a wave is measured from the bottom of its *trough*—the depression just in front of and behind each wave—to its crest. *Wavelength* refers to the horizontal distance between each crest, and *period* is the time between the passing of each crest.

Fortunately, waves in the temperate regions rarely reach the size of the southern monsters. In the Pacific Ocean off the west coast of North America, swells 5 to 15 feet high are normal and, provided they're not breaking, can be ridden effortlessly by a sea kayaker. A swell can move a lot of water up and down, but very little sideways. A kayaker riding a swell moves in a slightly elliptical pattern: up and forward a bit as the wave crest approaches, then down and back as it passes.

A breaking wave, however, releases vastly more energy than a swell. Normally, breaking waves are formed when a swell enters shallow water, such as when it approaches a shore. When the depth of the water diminishes to about half the wavelength, the friction of the substrate on the bottom of the wave begins to steepen its face—the wave is, in effect, leaning forward. When the depth diminishes to about 1 ½ times the wave height, the wave begins to *break*—that is, the face steepens to the point that it falls over. Our formerly benign swell is now dumping tons of water per second over anything in its path—surfers, kayakers, California beachfront homes. . . .

Waves away from a shore can break, too, when the wind blows hard enough to steepen their faces beyond the point of stability. You can see this happen even in a harbor, when a powerful wind causes whitecaps on waves no more than a foot or two high. When the 75-foot storm waves of the open ocean start breaking in hurricane-force winds, they can snap large ships in two like breadsticks.

So what's a mere kayaker to do under the threat of such apocalyptic destruction? Answer: Try to avoid kayaking in 75-foot breaking waves. For lesser conditions, read on.

Ocean waves—just like sound waves and light waves—can reflect, refract, and bend. Waves hitting a cliff or jetty reflect back out, creating a very confused area of colliding crests that can extend 100 yards out to sea. Called *clapotis*, these colliding crests can shoot skyward much higher than the incoming waves. Paddlers

Waves reflecting off a jetty or cliff can create dangerous, confused conditions.

are well advised to steer clear of such conditions. Even though you might feel more exposed farther offshore, the nonbreaking swells of the open sea will be easier to negotiate than chaotic conditions closer in.

Waves entering a narrow harbor entrance refract around the headlands, so the surf line is spread out within the harbor in a fan shape, even out of the direct line of the entrance (although their force is also diminished as they spread). Waves can also refract around a small island from both ends, resulting in colliding seas in the lee of the island—right where you'd expect calm water. Only very close inshore on the lee side will the seas flatten. You should note such patterns whenever you're out paddling; soon you'll become good at estimating sea patterns and conditions in most circumstances.

LAUNCHING AND LANDING THROUGH SURF

It's always great if you can launch and land in a sheltered harbor, but obviously things sometimes don't work that way. Nevertheless, launching and landing through moderate, 3- to 4-foot-high surf can become routine with practice and careful analysis of conditions. For starters, I recommend practicing in surf that's no more than 2 feet high.

The first thing to look for is a beach where the surf is spilling rather than dumping. *Spilling* surf occurs over a gently sloping bottom. The waves break rather gradually, and fairly far offshore; there's an area of foamy but relatively calm water between the shore and the main break, called *soup,* where you can easily launch and wait for the right time to punch through the break.

Dumping surf is a characteristic of steep shores, where the waves don't break until they're virtually on the beach. The break is

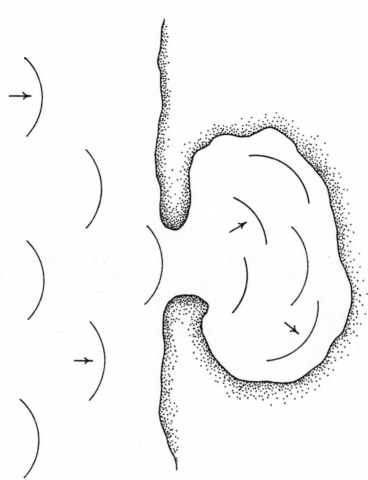

Waves entering a harbor refract around the headlands, creating surf even away from the direct line of the opening.

usually very steep and abrupt, the waves pounding the beach with heavy, shocklike sounds. Dumping surf is very dangerous, even when it's only a couple of feet high, and should be avoided at all costs.

Even on a beach with gently spilling surf, some areas will be calmer than others. Observe the break carefully and pick the spot where it's smallest. Then watch the wave sets.

Waves always occur in *sets*—a group of around seven, followed by a lull or at least a reduction in height for the next two or three waves. The idea is to time your launch so you reach the break just as a lull has arrived. Position your kayak at the water's edge and get set up. Make sure nothing on deck can be swept off; if you're wearing sunglasses, stash them somewhere dry until you launch or they'll quickly be obscured by salt residue.

If there's enough soup that you can launch and hold position just inside the break line, do so. Watch the surf through several sets to get a good idea of their timing and number. Then, when the last wave of a set has just broken and the smaller interim waves are on their way in, paddle swiftly straight out through them. You might make it past the surf without even encountering a breaking wave; however, if one does curl up at you, lean forward and punch right through it. It's a good idea to point your paddle straight ahead just as you go through the wave, so it doesn't get whacked into your chest by the wave, but be ready to paddle strongly immediately after the crest has passed. Also be ready to use rudder and paddle to maintain a straight line if the wave tries to knock your bow off course.

As you become more proficient at this technique and challenge bigger surf, your technique must change just a bit. When a large wave is curling toward you, you don't want the bow of your kayak to bury itself in the face, which will result in the wave engulfing you. The proper procedure is to lean *back* just as the bow begins to carve into the face—to unload the front of the boat and give it more buoyancy—then quickly lean forward again to help force the bow down through the crest of the wave. You must have a really good head of steam up to maintain the necessary momentum to punch through larger waves. Keep paddling strongly until you're well past the break line.

Now that I've gotten you out through the surf, let me bring up an important axiom: It's easier to launch through surf than it is to land through it. Right—the time to think about this is *before* you've launched. If you have any doubts at all about your ability to get out through the break, and you are not absolutely certain you have a more sheltered spot in which to land, don't go out, because it's going to be harder to get back in.

As with launchings, you'll want to time your landings to coincide with the lulls between sets. However, it's more difficult to observe sets from the seaward side. The best way is to slowly ease your way shoreward until you're just outside the point at which the

This paddler has spotted a break in the wave sets and is paddling out strongly through the lull.

waves are starting to curl. Be careful, because occasionally a wave will break farther out than the rest and catch you unawares. From this point you can usually tell—by the sound of waves breaking ahead of you, by the feel of the kayak moving up and down, and by watching seaward—how the sets are timed. As the last swell of a big set passes under you, paddle like crazy toward shore on the back of it. If everything works perfectly, you can ride right through the break line on the back of the wave even as its face curls and breaks in front of you, sending a welter of foam up around the bow.

During a lull in a series of 4-foot waves, the surf might be only a couple of feet high.

(a)

(b)

Often as not it *won't* work perfectly. What usually happens is that the wave outdistances you, and you're left floundering in the trough. Don't despair—keep paddling until the next wave catches up with you. At this point one of two things will occur. If you can keep the bow of the kayak pointed straight toward shore, the wave will overtake and lift you, and the kayak will rush toward shore as it planes down the face of the wave. Sometimes you can ride a wave all the way to shore; other times the wave will outdistance you again and you'll try to catch the following one.

A more likely scenario is that, as the wave overtakes and lifts you, the kayak will *broach;* that is, the stern will snap around one direction or the other so that the boat is parallel to the wave crest, bouncing along in roiling whitewater. This is okay—in fact in big surf it's almost inevitable. Just remember to immediately lean *into* the wave (rather than recoiling away from it as your instincts demand, which will instantly capsize you).

Remember the low brace? Now is the time to employ a *high* brace. Plant your paddle blade horizontally into the top of the wave and lean on it, with the shaft level with your shoulders or even higher if necessary. You'll find that the constant uplift of the water by the wave results in surprisingly firm support. In this position— leaning into the wave with a high brace—you can often ride the wave all the way in until it collapses and leaves you floating in the soup. If so, turn and paddle toward shore to escape the next wave. If the crest passes you, stop leaning as it does so, then use your rudder and/or a sweep stroke to turn toward shore again and race the next crest.

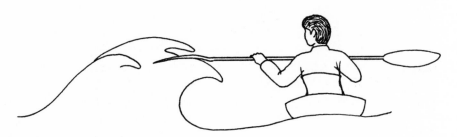

Demonstration of a high brace.

Sometimes a broach will happen slowly enough that you can feel it coming and turn out of it with the rudder, but at all times be ready to brace strongly if the boat starts to tip.

PADDLING IN WIND AND WAVES

It's perfectly possible to find yourself paddling in a high wind with flat seas, or in high waves with no wind at all. However, the two usually come together, so I'm going to deal with them at once and leave you to modify your tactics to suit the conditions.

An experienced sea kayaker can challenge conditions that would have many small sailboats and powered craft running for shelter. The kayak's relatively small size means that it presents less surface area for the wind to catch, bobbing over waves that might swamp a bigger boat. Your job is simply to keep the boat upright and headed in the right direction through all this.

Headwinds

Winds and waves coming directly toward the bow are, in many ways, the easiest to deal with—although they're also the most difficult to make any progress against.

Waves coming directly toward you naturally roll under the boat; often the worst you'll experience is a wild up-and-down ride as the kayak tips steeply up the face of each wave and then careens down the back, like a continuous surf launch. It can be quite fun. Heading into the wind is less of a problem as well; since you're presenting the smallest possible boat-paddler surface area, you can't very well be blown over backward.

The best way to handle headwinds and seas is to be aggressive. Lean forward and paddle hard. The wind will constantly attempt to force the bow off course, but it's easier to push ahead, keeping the boat straight rather than letting it get sideways and then trying to correct. If you're using a feathered paddle, you'll notice how much better the blades slice through the air; if it's not feathered, you'll have to force each blade forward.

Sometimes the waves will be steep enough that the bow tries to bury itself in their faces. Use the same techniques as for surf launchings: Lean back to help lift the bow over the wave, then quickly forward again to punch over the crest. If the backs of the waves are steep enough, you'll also experience some vertiginous free falls as the bow and two-thirds of the kayak hang in midair before crashing back into the water.

Paddling upwind is tiring, and the temptation to rest will be strong. But as soon as you stop paddling you'll start losing ground, which will tire you even more to regain. A sea anchor is the solution; it nearly eliminates backsliding and controls the boat so you can get a drink or snack without the constant need for corrective strokes. (See chapter 4, page 90.)

Downwind Paddling

Paddling with the wind is something of a dual-personality activity. In mild to moderate breezes you can really rip along—although it won't seem like you're going fast, because the seas and wind are with you; you need a nearby shore to mark your progress. I've covered 20 miles in a morning with minimal effort when a friendly 15-knot breeze kept up a steady pressure on my back; had I been using a sail, I could have added another 10 miles.

When the breeze and seas kick up, however, boat control becomes more difficult. If paddling in strong headwinds can be likened to a continuous surf launching, then paddling downwind in the same conditions is akin to a continuous surf landing, with waves coming up from behind, overtaking you, and trying to broach the kayak. You get a few wild rides surfing down the faces, but the troughs seem to suck you downward and backward, killing your momentum and diminishing your directional control.

If you've been enjoying an effortless morning of downwind paddling in light airs, but the breeze starts stiffening enough for you to feel the kayak trying to broach as waves pass, and the boat tilts farther and farther forward as the crests lift the stern, so that the bow digs deeper into the troughs of the waves in front, it's time to apply some corrective measures. Surprisingly, the first of these is to *paddle faster*. The faster your boat is moving through the water, the more directional control you'll have with the rudder. But beware: Steep waves can lift the stern and rudder completely out of the water, at which instant your rudder control vanishes and the boat will rapidly broach. If the waves are steep enough for this to happen, be ready for it. Don't kick the rudder over farther in a vain attempt to rudder thin air, because when it reenters the water the sudden grab will violently jerk the boat, possibly resulting in a capsize. Use a sweep stroke to maintain your desired heading as closely as possible, while being ready to brace if the boat starts to tip. Take advantage of the crests—with the ends of the boat out of the water, a sweep stroke will turn you very quickly if you need to adjust course.

If you can paddle fast enough to more or less keep up with the waves, you'll retain decent control. If the boat begins to surf down the face of a wave, use the rudder, or a paddle rudder stroke, to keep it headed downwind. If the waves are too steep to surf straight down, you can *tack*—angle down the face of one wave, then angle in the opposite direction down the next, maintaining your desired heading through a series of zigzag moves.

If the waves are moving too fast too keep up with, relax a bit and let the wind do most of the work of carrying you forward; meanwhile you can use your paddle largely for boat control, to maintain a downwind course. As the boat surfs, it will pick up speed and you can rudder to stay on line; once the crest passes, the boat will wallow and you can use a sweep to get the bow back on track.

What if conditions get really bad, but your only choice is to continue downwind? You might be better off turning the boat to face into the wind and letting it blow you backward. It's much easier to keep a kayak headed on course into the wind than away from it, and although your progress will slower, it will be safer.

The usual advice for making a 180-degree turn in wind is to pivot the kayak while it's on top of a wave or swell crest. This works for minor course adjustments, but it's almost impossible to turn a kayak completely around on one crest. Do it in stages—a sweep on the first crest might get you turned halfway, then you can hunker down in the trough and sweep again as the next crest passes. Remember that while you're sideways on the very top of a wave, you'll be exposed to the full force of the wind.

Crosswinds

A kayak left bobbing in the ocean by itself will normally assume a position perpendicular to the wind and parallel to waves; this is the only attitude in which all the forces acting on the boat are equalized. And you might think this would make it easy to paddle a kayak in a crosswind while maintaining a course—but an annoying bit of hydrodynamic physics gets in the way. As soon as you try to paddle a kayak straight across the wind, the boat tries to turn *upwind.* This is because as the boat moves through the water, the water pressure on the downwind side of the bow is greater than that on the downwind side of the stern, so the stern gets blown farther downwind. The tendency to turn upwind is called *weathercocking* ("weather helm" in sailing terms—as opposed to "lee helm," a tendency to turn downwind). Virtually all kayaks weathercock to a greater or lesser degree. If you just continue paddling without attempting any correcting strokes, the kayak will eventually settle on a course that's roughly 30 to 50 degrees away from straight upwind. In a kayak with a rudder or skeg, weathercocking is easy to correct: With a rudder, you just push on the downwind pedal a bit; if you have a skeg, now is the time to drop it. You'll have to experiment with how far to drop the blade to neutralize the handling.

I might as well tell you right now—paddling in strong side winds and heavy beam seas is no fun if you're trying to get somewhere (if you're just out playing it's a different story). The wind is trying to blow you over sideways, and the waves insist on slapping you rudely upside the head. The solution is to get pushy right back—and to resign yourself to getting wet. Keep a low profile by leaning forward and keeping your paddling stroke very low. In this situation unfeathered paddles have the advantage. Picture a feathered blade out of the water on its forward stroke: As soon as you lift it up it becomes an air scoop, and the wind tries to flip the paddle out of your grasp. An unfeathered paddle is easier to control.

Take care with your paddle strokes in beam seas. The best technique is to plant a forward stroke in the face of a wave as it approaches you, and then stroke into the back of it as it passes on the other side. If you try to stroke while poised on the crest of the wave, your paddle might meet thin air. This technique also allows you to convert to a bracing stroke if needed. If the waves are far enough apart you can take several strokes while you're in the trough, then one stroke on the face, one on the back, then several more in the trough. You'll soon develop a rhythm for the conditions.

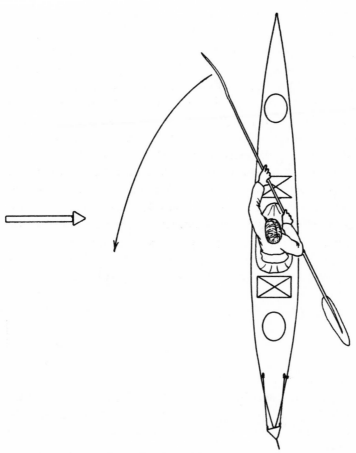

Using a sweep stroke and right rudder to compensate for wind coming from the left.

The hip movements I discussed in chapter 3 are vital in beam seas. You'll be gyrating like Elvis in an attempt to keep the boat essentially level with the horizon. Remember to keep your torso upright, so your center of gravity stays over the center of the boat, and the chance of capsizing will be minimal.

If the wind gets really nasty you might find yourself having to lean into it to maintain balance. If so, take care, because any sudden momentary cessation in the breeze will put you off balance. Be ready to brace.

Quartering Seas

Maintaining course in quartering seas is probably the trickiest of paddling techniques. A *quartering* wind (or wave) is one that's coming from somewhere between straight ahead and straight to the side, or between straight to the side and dead astern. In these situations you're essentially being forced to deal with elements of both headwinds and side winds, or following winds and side winds.

If possible, I often "square the circle" in nasty quartering seas—I'll paddle straight downwind or upwind until I can turn and paddle straight across the wind to my goal. If this tack isn't possible I pay very close attention to waves, especially those coming from behind me. Quartering waves from astern are particularly obnoxious, since it seems you've barely stopped leaning into the back of the one passing off the angle of your bow when you have to lean the other way for the one coming up on the opposite angle of the stern. Keep your hips limber and your knees locked under the deck so you can tilt the boat instantly.

CURRENTS

Often, currents present nothing more than a navigational challenge, which is why I'll deal with them in the next chapter as well. However, strong currents can create their own sea conditions, and when they collide with existing wind or waves very confused and unpredictable seas are the result.

The edges of currents can be easy to spot, because sea conditions often change noticeably—sometimes eerily—within just a few feet. A calm paddle will suddenly turn bouncy as a current stirs up the water. Or sometimes the opposite will happen: A current can dampen waves if it is going the same direction. Be extremely cautious of these juxtaposed conditions, since the current can grab the bow of your kayak as you enter the interface and actually affect your balance.

Be cautious of currents that are forced through a narrow strait or around a headland; they will pick up a considerable amount of speed. Be extremely cautious of currents that are colliding with a wind coming from the opposite direction. Such a situation will create steep, confused seas with little or no pattern.

PUTTING IT ALL TOGETHER

There will come times in your paddling career when all your skills will come into play at once. If you've practiced in controlled conditions and gradually extended your limits, you'll be ready.

For me one of those times occurred in the Sea of Cortez, when I was attempting a crossing from mainland Mexico to Baja California by hopping from island to island across the mid-rift chain of Tiburon, San Esteban, and San Lorenzo. I'd reached San Esteban and was paddling along its southern coast when I noticed that the sea to the south, out of the lee of the island, was looking increasingly rough. Nevertheless, I paddled out beyond the spit at the far southwestern corner of the island to have a look.

It was immediately obvious that I was going no farther that day. An incoming, northbound tide was slamming into a northerly (southbound) wind that had come up within the past 15 minutes, and the seas were chaotic, with breaking crests falling in random directions and a 35-knot wind blowing spume off the water.

The wind essentially sucked my kayak right out into the open water; when I looked back the spit seemed impossibly far off. So I decided to run with the seas to get back into the lee of the island. I turned the kayak around to point southeast and paddled hard, surfing wildly on the steep wave faces, angling east when the wave sets diminished momentarily and I could turn the boat on the crests. Within 10 minutes I was directly downwind of the island— but a good mile away, so quickly had the wind carried me even over the tidal current. Again using succeeding wave crests, I turned the kayak around once more and slogged upwind toward the island, keeping my head down and paddling strongly. It took me 45 minutes to regain the relatively calm water near land, and the last 100 yards were the roughest of all, as wind gusts curving off the cliffs on the island punched straight down on me. I was exhausted, but satisfied, when I landed on the spit. I had faced nearly every condition a kayaker could expect within the previous hour, but I'd known what to do and had done it satisfactorily.

It might be a long time before you face similar conditions in open water. And if I'd been smart enough to land and climb the spit to check conditions, I might have avoided it myself!) But if you take the time to practice rough-weather techniques in controlled conditions, you'll be well prepared if you're ever caught out unexpectedly.

CHAPTER 6

NAVIGATION AND SEAMANSHIP

It might sound unlikely, but coastal route-finding is an excellent way to learn the fundamentals of navigation. The reason is that unlike inland orienteering (or offshore navigation), your scope for error is reduced to a single, one-dimensional line—the interface between water and land. The worst that can happen to your calculations is that you end up farther up or farther down the coast than you thought.

FINDING YOUR WAY

Charts

A chart is simply a map of the ocean. While some terrestrial features are included—especially hills, rivers, and other landmarks that might serve as aids to navigation—most of the information deals with the sea and its boundaries. Depths, current speeds, and tidal ranges are shown, as well as extremely detailed representations of coastlines, islands, and harbors, along with artificial navigational aids such as lighthouses and buoys. Everything is as precise as possible, because the information could literally mean life or

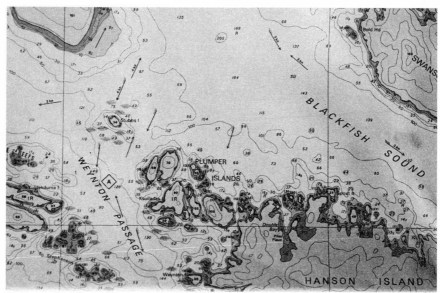

Section of a chart, showing depths and currents.

death to a ship or yacht captain relying on the chart to navigate through fog or dark of night.

Much of the information on a chart might seem like overkill for a sea kayaker, but in fact charts are just as useful on a 17-foot kayak as they are on a 500-foot freighter. Tidal currents, for example, depending on their strength, can be used by a paddler to gain a boost in speed along a coast, or can create dangerous conditions to be avoided. Your chart will list peak current speed and direction to help you pick the proper strategy. A narrow channel that decreases in depth from 120 to 30 feet along its length might seem to make no difference to a kayak with a 6-inch draft, but a current moving down that channel will increase in speed as it's squeezed over the shallow end, and the volume of water being forced through a smaller space can create hazardous standing waves and whirlpools. If you have a chart, you can predict this in advance and time your passage to miss the peak current flow. And at its most basic, a chart is invaluable for determining distances and directions—extremely difficult to estimate from a vantage point only 3 feet off the water.

To pinpoint your location on a chart you utilize universal lines of position—longitude and latitude—which divide up the globe into degrees, and are further divided into minutes and seconds. Lines of longitude circle the earth from pole to pole, like the segments of an orange. Lines of longitude are farthest apart at the equator, and converge at each pole. The reference point, 0 degrees, runs through Greenwich, England; from there the lines run west, toward the United States, and east, toward Asia, until they meet in the Pacific on the opposite side of the world from England, at 180 degrees (the international date line). Thus a point in the U.S. might be at 110 degrees west longitude; if you traveled the same distance the other direction from Greenwich, you'd find yourself at 110 degrees east longitude.

Lines of latitude run perpendicular to lines of longitude, starting with the equator at 0 degrees and forming smaller and smaller concentric circles until they reach the South Pole at 90 degrees south, and the North Pole at 90 degrees north. Unlike lines of longitude, lines of latitude are parallel to each other, so they are always the same distance apart.

Degrees (indicated by the symbol °) of longitude and latitude are divided into minutes ($\frac{1}{60}$ of 1 degree, indicated by '), and seconds ($\frac{1}{60}$ of 1 minute, indicated by "). One minute of latitude, equal to about 1.15 land (or "statute") miles, is known as a *nautical mile*. A knot, referring to the speed of a boat, is 1 nautical mile per hour, or about 1.15 land miles per hour. Longitude cannot be used to reckon distance the same way, since the distance between lines of longitude varies—at the equator a minute of longitude covers about the same distance as a minute of latitude; within a few feet of the North or South Poles, though, a minute of longitude represents only a fraction of an inch!

Any point on earth can be described to within about 100 feet using lines of position. When listing map or chart coordinates, latitude is always given first: for example, 47°59'07" N, 122°11'10" W. If you have a very accurate map, you'll find that this describes a spot in downtown Everett, Washington.

Charts and maps are usually inscribed across their faces with major lines of position; the coordinates are listed in the margin.

One source of confusion for many people is the "scale" of the chart, which can be referred to as small scale or large scale. But does "small scale" mean that the chart covers a small area, resulting in greater detail, or that it shows more area and the *features* are smaller, so that there's less detail? Actually the latter is the case. I remember the difference with a mnemonic device that uses the word S.C.A.L.E.: Small-scale Covers A Large arEa (yeah, yeah, I know, it's not perfect, but it works). Most kayakers use large-scale charts of around 1:20,000—that is, 1 inch on the chart equals 20,000 inches, or about $^3/_{10}$ of a mile on the sea. Small-scale charts of 1:250,000 or so are more suitable for rough trip planning.

A good companion to your chart is a *nautical chart index*, which translates all those confusing chart symbols into usable information.

Compasses

Life would be so simple for the navigator if compass needles pointed toward true north, the geographic north pole, where the lines of longitude converge and toward which all maps are oriented. Unfortunately, the compass needle is attracted to the *magnetic* north pole, which is several hundred miles away, northwest of Baffin Island in the Canadian Arctic. (As if that weren't enough, the magnetic pole moves over time; when the first explorers searched for the Northwest Passage, their rudimentary compasses pointed in a significantly different direction than ours.)

Fortunately, the difference between where the compass tells you north is and its real location is easy to figure—and sometimes you don't even have to worry about it.

Directions on maps and charts are divided up into 360 degrees. True north is 0 degrees, east is 90, south is 180, and west is 270. Just as with lines of position, this allows very precise descriptions of a course or direction to an object—for instance, a buoy that's a bit south of due east of you might be at 95 degrees, and so on. Remember, on all charts and maps directions are oriented with geographic north.

However, somewhere on the page will be a symbol listing the *variation* (if on a chart) or *declination* (if a map). This is the difference, for the region shown on the sheet, between true north and magnetic north, in degrees. *Variation* and *declination* mean exactly the same thing, and I have no clue as to why cartographers decided

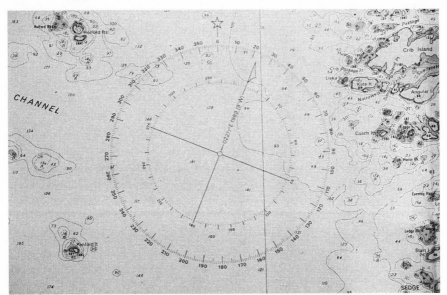

A key showing the variation on a chart.

to confuse us with such capriciousness. For my hometown of Tucson, Arizona, the *declination* (since I'm looking at a *map*) is 13 degrees east; that is, my compass needle points 13 degrees east of true north. In the Pacific Northwest, declination is around 22 degrees east. In some places on earth, of course—those where the magnetic north pole is directly between the observer and the geographic north pole (or directly on the other side)—the declination is 0 degrees, and no compensation is needed. In other areas, such as places in the high Arctic, it might be over 90 degrees.

So how do you compensate for this variation while kayaking? One answer is that sometimes you don't have to. For example, if you're kayaking with a friend and you see an island you want to head for, you point your boat at it and look at the *lubber line* on your compass—the line that tells you which way your kayak is headed. If the line says the island is at 30 degrees, you tell your friend, "Let's head for that island at 30 degrees." Simple—no compensation is needed, because you're both working strictly from the compass. This type of heading is called a *magnetic bearing*. The variation is irrelevant—unless you want to look at your chart and identify which island it is you're headed toward. Then you need to convert your magnetic bearing to a true bearing. Let's say you're paddling from a harbor, the location of which you know. Locate the harbor on the chart, then look for the variation symbol, which in this case we'll say lists variation at 10 degrees east. That means if you take a magnetic bearing for north (0 degrees), your compass is actually pointing at 10 degrees true. So your magnetic bearing of 30 degrees to the island is really at 40 degrees true. To find out what island you're looking at, you place a protractor or a handheld orienteering compass on your chart, with the hub over your present position in the harbor and the 0-degree mark pointed toward true north. Then extend an imaginary line on the chart out through the 40-degree mark until you hit an island—that will be the island you're looking at.

You can work backward if you want to visually locate the same island after finding it on the chart first. Just take your 40-degree true bearing and subtract the variation, then point your kayak and boat compass at the resulting magnetic bearing.

If you're in an area where the variation is west instead of east, you have to reverse the above instructions: *Add* the variation to a true bearing to get the magnetic heading, and *subtract* it from a magnetic bearing to get the true heading. It sounds ridiculously convoluted, but you'll find that in practice it becomes second nature—particularly since, in a kayak, you're not going to be swapping from east variation to west variation on any one trip (unless it's a real epic), so you only have to memorize one formula at a time.

Your boat compass has no easy means for compensating for variation, but most good handheld compasses have an adjustable variation arrow under the needle. You set the arrow so it points toward the degree of variation on the compass dial; then, if you hold the compass so the needle floats directly over the arrow, the dial is oriented toward true north. To take a bearing with a handheld compass, you essentially hold it in one position, with the 0-degree mark pointed north, and rotate *yourself* around the compass until you're looking at your target over the compass, and can look down to see which degree mark is pointing the way you are. If the compass has a baseplate with a bearing arrow, you rotate the plate until the arrow points toward your desired bearing, adding precision to the reading. And if you have a really good compass, it will

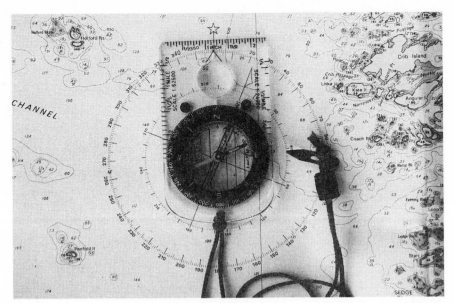

Adjust the variation arrow on your handheld compass to match the variation on the chart.

have a mirror over the dial, which allows you to hold the compass at eye level for extremely accurate bearings.

For a much more in-depth look at route-finding for paddlers, I recommend David Burch's *Fundamentals of Kayak Navigation* (see appendix 2).

GPS Units

Now that handheld Global Positioning Satellite units can be had for less than the price of a good dinner out, more and more kayakers are carrying them. And that's fine—up to a point.

GPS units read the signals from an orbiting network of satellites, and can locate the user's position anywhere on the globe to within a 100 feet or so, sometimes much less. The reason for the disparity is something called selective availability, which is a random inaccuracy programmed into the system for national security reasons. However, even with selective availability the capabilities of

GPS units are awesome (and I hear that the selective availability scrambling might be ended soon).

Still, to be frank, most kayakers who carry GPS units do so more for their toy value than for any practical advantage on a normal paddling trip. If you rely on them for genuine route-finding through areas where becoming lost is a real possibility, keep in mind that they are electronic devices subject to failure like any other such tool. I would never use a GPS unit without solid chart skills as a backup, and would constantly check my GPS readings with compass bearings.

Most GPS units have extra functions such as speed calculation, graphic course representation, and ETA. But the sampling time needed for such functions is somewhat short given the speed at which a kayaker typically travels, so the readings can be inaccurate.

SEAMANSHIP

Seamanship, with apologies to gender-neutral etymological revisionists (no substitute term could possibly evoke the same image), refers to the complete range of skills necessary for dealing with the sea and all her . . . whoops, its . . . moods. While a book can offer advice on currents, waves, and so forth, only experience will give you the instinct to read myriad conditions automatically: to know at a glance how fast a current is running—and whether it's navigable; whether a shore break offers a safe landing; how far away an oncoming ship is and how soon it will present a hazard; whether a beam sea is too steep to fight; and on and on. Paddling a sea kayak puts you on an accelerated curve toward such skills, however, because of the intimate relationship that always exists between a small craft and the water.

The single most important facet of seamanship is a combination of good judgment, common sense, and caution. Knowing your own limits is part of this combination. Never, ever, let someone else talk you into paddling in conditions in which you're not comfortable. Never let other outside influences—plane schedules, rain clouds, being late for dinner—push you into paddling when or where you shouldn't. The obvious corollary is Don't ever try to talk others into paddling when they don't want to, and don't ridicule them for the decision, no matter how benign conditions appear to you.

Tidal Currents

Virtually all currents kayakers must deal with are created by tides. A *tide* is simply a bulge of water pulled up from the earth's surface by the gravitational pull of the moon and, to a lesser extent, the sun. In essence, the earth rotates *under* the bulge of water, and when the bulge hits a landmass the result is a rise in the water level, from a few inches in many areas to over 40 feet in a couple of places, such as the Bay of Fundy in Nova Scotia. A tidal rise of just a few feet can create significant currents if all that water is squeezed between an island and the mainland, for instance, or even around a peninsula or point jutting out into the ocean.

Most coastlines experience two high tides and two low tides each day (although there are exceptions). The actual period is about 24 hours and 50 minutes, which is the time it takes for the moon to appear in the same place in the sky each day. Thus a high tide is followed in about six hours by a low tide, and so on. Why two whole up-and-down cycles when there's only one moon? Not, as you might think, because of the sun's influence, but because the moon actually pulls the earth enough to create a little bit of a wobble in its rotation. So as the moon pulls up a tidal bulge, it pulls the earth, too, which leaves another, smaller, tidal bulge sticking out on the opposite side of the globe. Tides are biggest—that is, the variation between low and high tide is the largest—when the moon and the sun are on the same side of the earth, pulling together (this is the period of the new moon, when only a sliver of moon is visible near sunset or sunrise), or when the moon and sun are opposed (during the full moon). Tidal variation is smallest between these two periods (quarter moon). The new- and full-moon tides are called *spring tides;* the modest quarter-moon tides are called *neap tides*. While we're covering terminology, an incoming tide is *flooding;* an outgoing tide is *ebbing*.

Tidal charts are available for most paddling areas and will tell you when high and low tides occur, as well as their expected range. You can time your paddling either to take advantage of tidal currents going your way, if they're not too strong, or to avoid the

Narrow channels, such as this one in the Sea of Cortez, are subject to strong tidal currents. Note the shifting sandbars.

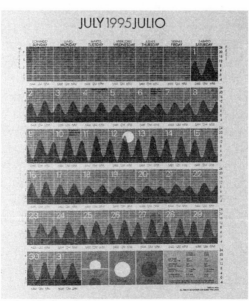

Tidal charts are invaluable for planning any outing. Graphs such as this are easier to read than those showing only numbers.

strongest periods of flow. Books called coastal pilots contain detailed information about tides and their effects along many coasts, and are worth buying for multiday trips.

Beware any areas of strong tidal currents shown on your chart. If you need to negotiate a narrow strait or paddle around a point where the tidal current exceeds 1 or 2 knots, time your paddle for *slack water,* the period of slowest flow; this occurs, contrary to what you might think, right around the highest and lowest water levels. The current is moving fastest about halfway between high and low tides.

If you have to cross a channel through which a current is flowing and you aim straight across at your target, you'll be constantly swept off course by the current—even as you continue to point your bow toward your destination—until, as you near the opposite shore, you suddenly realize that your heading has changed so you are now forced to paddle directly upstream, as it were, to reach your goal. It's better to compensate for the current from the start. If the channel is narrow you might be able to complete the entire crossing during slack water; alternatively, you can begin the crossing near the end of the incoming (or outgoing) flow, paddle through slack water, and reach the other side shortly after the opposite flow has begun, thus counteracting the drift. However, if you cannot wait out the current you'll just have to maneuver with it, by pointing the boat upstream from your intended target. It feels completely wrong at first to be paddling in the wrong direction, but you'll get there much sooner.

The problem is judging just how far upstream to point the bow if you're to maintain a straight course across the current. One of the easiest ways to stay on track is to use *leading marks*. These can be almost any two objects that are both easily seen and in line with each other when you begin your crossing. Let's say you're crossing a channel to a harbor, and you can see a tall sailboat mast in the harbor along with a dead pine tree on the hill directly behind it. The current is flowing from your left to your right, so you aim your bow 20 or 30 degrees to the left of the harbor and begin paddling. Keep an eye on the mast and tree—if the mast begins drifting to the left of the tree, you're being swept downcurrent and should either paddle faster or aim the bow farther upcurrent. If the mast moves to the right of the tree, you're overcompensating and can aim a bit straighter.

Make sure your leading marks are distinctive; it does no good to pick out a sailboat mast in a harbor full of masts unless there's something really unique about one of them.

Shipping Hazards

Most people know, in some abstract sense, that a kayak is a difficult thing to see from the deck of a large ship, but few realize just how difficult. As far as big ships are concerned, consider that the skipper of an average-size freighter can't see *anything* within about 1,000 feet of the ship's bow—the view is completely blocked by the hull. And beyond that distance a kayaker is just not there at all. Combine this with the fact that a large ship requires over $1/2$ mile to make an emergency stop, and nearly as much to make an abrupt 90-degree turn, and you can easily infer the lesson: Stay out of the way of big ships.

Fortunately, large ships stay in recognized shipping lanes (frequently illustrated on charts) when they're near land, so it's easy to predict their movements. Normally there's no reason on earth for a kayaker to paddle in a shipping lane; however, now and then it's necessary to *cross* one, a situation akin to a mouse attempting to gain the opposite side of a busy freeway.

First look at your chart, and determine the width of the channel you need to cover. Figure your paddling speed; for most kayakers this is about 3 knots (roughly 3.5 miles per hour) at a normal pace, or 5 knots or so under imminent fear of death. When you've determined about how long it will take you to cross to safety, time several ships from the moment they appear until they pass by your position. This will give you your window of opportunity. You'll notice that big ships seem hardly to move when they're on the horizon, then gain speed with frightening swiftness as they grow nearer. Sometimes you can determine more or less where the borders of the shipping lane are (often they're marked with buoys), and gain a little time by paddling to the edge and waiting for a clear space. Do not dally once you are in the lane, even if nothing is visible. Some high-powered monstrosity could appear traveling at twice the speed of everything else you timed.

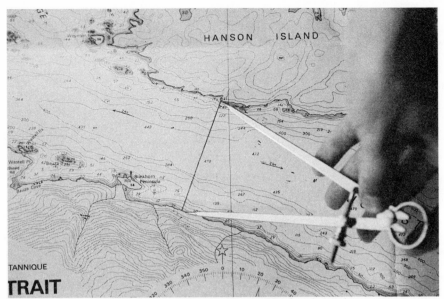

Use a set of dividers or a ruler to measure the width of a channel.

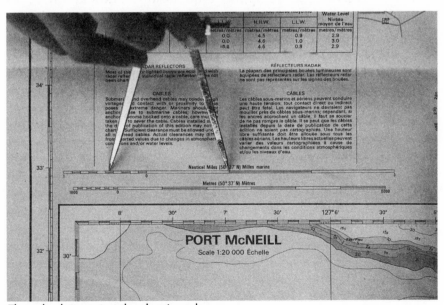

Then check it against the chart's scale.

It's up to you to stay out of the way of large ships.

A greater hazard to the kayaker probably lies with small sail and power vessels, which can maneuver unexpectedly, can turn nearly as quickly as you, are several times faster—and will often be traveling the same routes as you. The overriding axiom is to never, ever, assume that the other craft has seen you. I've been nearly run down on more than one occasion by boats whose skippers I swore had direct eye contact with me; the looks on their faces as we passed within feet of each other made it clear they had no idea I was there until they were on top of me.

If you find yourself in a possible interference situation with a power- or sailboat, try to turn broadside to it, offering your most visible area. Wave your paddle above your head with the blade facing the other boat. If all else fails and you cannot get out of the way of a boat that's changing course erratically and endangering you, consider firing a meteor flare across its bow; this might annoy the skipper, but it could save your life. Of course, if you're deliberately menaced by another craft, get its registration number and report it to the Coast Guard.

Keeping notes on your routes and paddling times will help you plan ahead.

Night and Fog

Paddling at night is one of my favorite experiences. Sitting quietly in a kayak, far out on a calm black sea with stars arcing overhead, offers a resoundingly peaceful counterpoint to the hectic minutiae on which we normally concentrate like furious communal insects.

On warm spring nights in the Sea of Cortez, when every paddle stroke sends a plume of green bioluminescence trailing from the boat, I have more than once paddled until dawn and slept through most of the following day because I couldn't tear myself away from the beauty.

But night paddling does, of course, demand caution, and your first experiences should be in sheltered and familiar waters. As difficult as a kayak is to see during the day, it's obviously invisible at night, so watching for other boat traffic is vital. You can show enough light to make yourself visible to larger craft, but that ruins your own night vision; I prefer to just stay out of boating channels.

Paddling at night with friends is fun, and you can strap a Cyalume stick on each paddler's rear deck, where it won't spoil anyone's vision but will help keep the group cohesive. You should each have a flashlight or headlamp in case more light is needed, and don't forget to leave some sort of light at your launch spot so you can find your way back.

When it's really dark, your ears will collect as much useful information as your eyes. Listen for the sound of water on the beach or offshore rocks, or of swells larger than the norm coming up on your boat.

If, for some unfortunate reason, you have to enter or cross a shipping channel at night, stop first and watch both ways for several minutes so that you can distinguish moving ship traffic from stationary shore lights. Remember that all vessels are required to show a red light on the port (left) side and a green light on the starboard (right) side, which must be visible from in front of and to the side of the ship, and a white masthead light (or two if the ship is longer than 165 feet).

While I enjoy paddling at night, I avoid fog if at all possible. Unlike darkness, fog completely eliminates visibility for both you and everyone else on the water, in addition to dampening sound and making it difficult to tell from which direction it's coming. If you paddle in an area where the possibility of being caught out in fast-moving fog is real, carry a foghorn; it will be your sole means of letting other boaters know you're there.

This electronic barometer has a surprisingly accurate forecasting function.

Weather

Sea kayakers deal with the weather on the most intimate level possible. Our needs go far beyond the weather report on the nightly news, even beyond the Weather Channel. We must incorporate both weather reports and our own observations to construct an informed strategy for each day's paddle.

The best weather reports for mariners are broadcast by the National Oceanic and Atmospheric Administration (NOAA). With a VHF radio you can tune in up-to-date reports on one of three channels in the United States; an additional channel is operated by the Coast Guard in Canada. Most VHF radios incorporate an automatic weather channel button, so you can switch instantly from any other channel to get a current report. You can also buy small radios that receive only weather channels, but I prefer the versatility of a two-way VHF transceiver.

Even the best broadcast reports, however, deal with areas far larger than concern a paddler. While the general information concerning high- and low-pressure systems, sea state, and wind patterns will certainly be useful, you need to pay close attention to what the weather is doing in your immediate area.

A handheld barometer is an excellent tool for predicting local trends. A *barometer* measures atmospheric pressure, which changes with elevation (an altimeter is just a barometer with elevation marked on it) and also with shifts in the weather—fair weather usually brings high pressure, while storms are accompanied by low pressure. The key for a paddler is the pressure *trend*. A falling barometer often presages bad weather; a rising barometer indicates clearing; a steady needle signifies steady conditions. Usually. I've found my barometer predictions to be about 75 percent accurate, which is a dang sight better than guessing.

Learn the local lore for your paddling area. For example, on trips in the Sea of Cortez I try to pick up southern California weather reports. If the forecast predicts Santa Ana winds, I can often expect a *Norte*—a steady northerly wind that can blow 20 knots for days on end—within 24 to 36 hours. It's caused in part by high-pressure winds from California draining down the natural funnel formed by the Sea of Cortez. The coastal pilot books for the area in which you're paddling will be a good source of regional weather trends.

CHAPTER 7

KAYAK CAMPING

When I began sea kayaking, I soon found that the very hardest maneuver to master was turning around. It didn't matter if I was exploring a cove, a crowded harbor, or a deserted coastline—I was always itching to see what was beyond the next point (or even beyond the next moored Hinckley). The solution came quickly: Throw a sleeping bag, tent, and food in the boat and just *keep going*.

If you've ever been backpacking, you'll take to kayak touring effortlessly; in fact, you'll be astonished at the luxury in which you can travel in a craft designed to carry 150 or 200 pounds of gear. No more filing down toothbrush handles or cutting the labels off tea bags to save weight.

However, even if you've never camped at all—or have only indulged in the euphemistic "camping" that involves space-shuttle-size vehicles equipped with satellite dishes and whirlpool bathtubs—you'll still find kayak camping an easy step. All that capacity is forgiving of those not yet used to traveling light (sorry—the satellite dish won't fit).

Backpacking equipment is perfectly suited for kayak touring. The compact tents, stoves, sleeping bags, and accessories designed for those who must carry it all on their backs have been honed over the years into efficient and reliable tools that waste neither space nor weight. Keep in mind, however, that some of the conditions you'll encounter as a kayaker are a little harder on gear than what most backpackers run into—salt air, stiff breezes, even the occasional dunking—so buy the best you can afford.

EQUIPMENT

Tent

If you're on a penny-squeezing budget and must economize on every piece of camping equipment but one, spend your money on a top-quality tent. Nothing has as much impact on your onshore comfort and safety as the delicate assembly of nylon and aluminum that serves as your home. You can even survive with a cheap sleeping bag as long as you've got a secure place to get out of the weather—and since coastal regions naturally tend toward the windy, you need something that will not only hold up but also let you get to sleep at night without a lot of flapping.

I used to lead kayaking trips, and I always cringed when clients unloaded those $39.95 dome tents with the spindly fiberglass poles. If there was any breeze at all, there was a good possibility that the tent would rip or a pole would break before it was even erected. And if it made it that far, the clients could look forward to a night with a tent wall draped over their faces as the thing leaned drunkenly in the wind. Fortunately, rain is uncommon in the Sea of Cortez, because the flies on these tents rarely proved more waterproof than a cotton T-shirt.

Be sure to buy your tent at a specialty store where knowledgeable salesclerks will help you find the right model for your needs. There are essentially two styles of tent dominating the market. The dome tent looks like what it's called; it's normally hemispherical, or nearly so. Its floor shape can be hexagonal or rectangular. Some domes have poles that all arc over the same point at the peak of the tent, like lines of longitude on a globe; others, called geodesic domes, use a pole structure that forms interconnected triangles. The latter style is usually more stable (although a good model with longitude-style poles might outperform a cheap geodesic model).

The other style of tent is the tunnel or hoop, which looks like a Conestoga wagon canopy, except that the foot end is generally lower to save weight and spill wind better. The poles can be parallel hoops, or might utilize a modified geodesic arrangement with several crossover points.

Dome tents are generally very roomy, since mathematically a hemisphere encloses more volume per square foot than other shapes. Domes also boast being "freestanding"—that is, they don't need stakes to stand up. This feature is overblown, however, since any tent should be staked down at all times. The best use I've found for the freestanding feature is picking up the tent every few days to shake out the sand.

Hoop tents, while smaller inside, are also lighter as a rule and thus a good choice if you backpack as well as kayak. Either design can be made sturdy enough to stand up to nasty weather.

A vital facet of how well a tent will stand up to wind is the tautness of the fabric. The fabric in the *canopy* (the body of the tent) and, to a lesser extent, the *fly* (the waterproof outer layer) is intrinsic to the structure. A well-cut canopy will distribute the force of wind throughout the entire tent, ensuring that no one pole or fabric panel is overly stressed. This is one of the biggest differences between bad tents and good tents, and is the first thing to look for when shopping. The fewer wrinkles showing on the floor model, the better (but look to see that the demonstrator is properly pitched; a poorly pitched tent will sages regardless of quality).

Make sure the tent is equipped with Easton aluminum poles. Fiberglass poles are a near-sure giveaway of an inferior tent. I've seen aluminum poles bent into horrifying shapes by storms and still emerge unscathed. Unfortunately, I've yet to find any tent that came with stakes worth a hoot. Throw out those wimpy skewers and buy a set of Black Diamond T-stakes, the large size. Buy extra ones so you can rig guylines for storms, and you'll sleep like a baby through the worst nature can throw at you.

Try out the tent to be sure it fits you. Ignore the maker's two-person, three-person designations and look at the floor space. For two people you'll want at least 30 square feet, and 35 or 40 is better, especially if you paddle in areas where you might be tentbound for any length of time. For rainy Northwest trips, my wife and I carry a North Face VE-25, which is luxurious for two at 47 square

A sturdy tent, such as this North Face VE-25, will guarantee a safe and dry night's sleep in any weather.

feet. I'm a big fan of vestibules, which give you a storage area for shoes and other such items out of the rain but out of the tent.

Brands? I like Marmot, The North Face, Mountain Hardwear, and Moss. For a very good tent on a budget, try Sierra Designs.

An excellent accessory for your tent is a waterproof nylon groundsheet cut to fit exactly under the tent floor, offered by many tent makers. These provide an extra waterproof layer for the floor, but more importantly they protect the tent floor from abrasion and add years to its life. You can make your own groundsheet from a nylon tarp, but make sure it doesn't stick out from under the floor; otherwise it will channel rainwater under the tent and *increase* the possibility of leakage instead of decreasing it.

Sleeping Bag

No matter what you hear to the contrary, no one has yet invented a sleeping bag fill material that will match top-quality goose down for warmth, light weight, and durability. While a goose-down bag might cost twice or even three times what a synthetic-fill bag will, the down bag will be more economical in the long run, since it will outlast the synthetic bag by a factor of three or four. A down bag will compress smaller than any synthetic bag of the same temperature rating, and will be a third lighter.

However—and this is a big *however*—goose down is absolutely worthless if it gets wet, and it dries at about the same rate trees grow unless you have access to a commercial Laundromat. This factor has led many sea kayakers—*many* meaning probably 99.5 percent—to choose a synthetic-fill sleeping bag for touring. And that's just fine, since synthetics have been getting better and better over the last decade. Virtually any of the highly hyped proprietary fills—Polarguard HV, Primaloft, et cetera, et cetera—will work just fine, and you can toss any of them in a home washing machine when it's dirty. A down bag needs a front-loading commercial machine (or hand washing) followed by about 50 quarters' worth of low-heat drying. If your synthetic bag gets soaked while kayaking, you can wring it out and regain a decent percentage of its efficiency—although it won't be very comfortable to sleep in until it thoroughly dries, in a day or two.

Sea kayakers are lucky—the characteristics of maritime climates usually result in mild nighttime temperatures along most paddling routes. A good "three-season" bag (meaning spring-summer-fall), good down to around 20 to 25 degrees F, will be adequate for most paddling. Keep in mind your own physique, however, and adjust what you buy accordingly. Women in general need warmer sleeping bags than men.

As for me, I carry an old Marmot rectangular sleeping bag filled with 625-inch goose down. It weighs 2 pounds exactly and compresses to the size of a 1-pound coffee can. It's 15 years old and still performing well, although it has lost probably an inch of loft and I'm thinking of having it refilled. For kayaking I put it inside a waterproof stuff sack, which I wrap in a plastic garbage bag and then put inside a heavy-duty dry bag. It has never gotten wet, and the Gore-Tex outer shell keeps damp coastal air and condensation out of the insulation. I use a cotton liner, which keeps the bag clean for long periods of time; when it does need washing I send it to a down-cleaning service that does it for me for not much money. It's been a good friend.

Sleeping Pad

A couple of decades ago, backpackers had to decide between the comfortable but bulky open-cell foam pad, the uncomfortable but reasonably compact closed-cell foam pad, or the very compact, reasonably comfortable, but puncture-prone air mattress.

All that changed with the invention of the self-inflating foam-filled sleeping pad, pioneered by Cascade Designs with its Therm-a-Rest model. Combining the comfort and insulative properties of air-supported foam with a tough outer shell, the Therm-a-Rest eclipses every other sleeping pad on the market. It works just great for kayaking as well, in addition to which you can choose one of the thicker models for even more comfort, since your kayak has more storage space than a backpack.

Although it's resistant to punctures, the Therm-a-Rest is not thornproof, so carry a patch kit. In very stickery areas, you might consider using an open-cell foam pad instead.

You can increase the utility of your Therm-a-Rest by about 1,000 percent by adding a Therm-a-Lounger to it. The Therm-a-Lounger (made by a different company, Crazy Creek) is a heavy nylon cover for the mattress (which makes it more puncture-resistant), with adjustable straps that convert it to an incredibly comfortable beach chair. A warning, though—if you're paddling with friends who don't have them, do not under any circumstances leave your Therm-a-Lounger unoccupied, or it will be appropriated.

One item considered a frivolity by many people—but not me—is a pillow. Not just a sack into which you can stuff a jacket, but a real foam or foam-and-air pillow. I found my sleep improved markedly when I began bringing along a foam pillow with an inflatable bladder inside. I blow it up firm for presleep reading, then deflate it to gentle support for the night.

Stoves and Cook Kits

Before you buy a stove for kayaking you'll first have to commit to which type of fuel to use. Liquid-fuel stoves burn white gas, and some can also use kerosene, automotive gas, and even diesel fuel.

Backpacking stoves make perfect sea-kayaking stoves.

Canister stoves burn liquefied petroleum (LP) gas such as isobutane or an isobutane-propane blend.

Liquid fuel is the most thermally efficient, and thus cheapest, fuel for stoves. It's also usually the hottest—meaning that a liquid-fuel stove will boil water quickly but not simmer too well (although MSR has recently improved the simmering capabilities of its stoves). For long trips, where fuel space is at a premium, or those on which you'll be cooking for a number of people, liquid fuel is the best way to go. But it's also messy, since it must be decanted from a container, and the priming needed for most stoves is a bit of a fuss.

With an LP stove, on the other hand, you just screw on a fuel cartridge, turn a valve, and light a match. Some even boast piezo-electric igniters, obviating even the match. There's no smell or spillage, there's less noise than with liquid fuel, and simmering is effortless. Fuel costs, however, are two to three times higher. There's also the problem of the empty cartridge, which with many stoves is destined to take up landfill space. Fortunately this is changing—the new Coleman Max Performance fuel cartridges are aluminum and can be crushed and recycled right along with your Coke cans.

My loyalties are divided. I use an LP stove for short trips, because of the convenience, and a liquid-fuel model for longer expeditions to conserve fuel. Soon I might not have to choose—a couple of companies are working on models that can be converted to run on either liquid or canister fuel. Smart.

Selection of pots and pans is one area where it's wise to deviate from the backpacking norm. Backpacking pots are designed for light weight above all other considerations; as a result they are thin and scorch food easily. I prefer heavier aluminum or stainless pots, preferably with removable handles to simplify storage. I like nonstick pots for easy cleanup; however, they preclude scrubbing with beach sand, one of the most effective natural cleaners you can find. A 1 $1/_2$- and a 2-liter pot are just about right for one or two people.

An utterly frivolous cooking toy that I now flatly refuse to travel without is the Outback Oven, sold by Cascade Designs. It's an effective and versatile oven system comprising a covered nonstick pan with a thermometer, a heat diffuser, and an aluminized fabric reflector cover. With an Outback Oven you can produce anything from fresh brownies to pizza. I've taken to carrying an extra stove on many trips so that I can bake dessert while I'm cooking dinner. You can use many grocery store mixes in the oven, although the proprietary mixes available from Cascade Designs are excellent, normally requiring only the addition of water.

If you like good coffee in the morning, you'll appreciate a double-wall stainless-steel mug like the one I've carried for years. It keeps any hot drink steaming for a long time. I use a small drip cone to brew coffee right into the cup. For a trip or two I carried a tiny, plastic hand-cranked coffee grinder and whole beans, but the thing proved so incredibly slow and difficult to use that I've reverted to grinding a trip's supply ahead of time at home.

Other useful kitchen items: a plastic cutting board—or, better, two—as big as you can manage. Vital for keeping sand out of the food prep, and great as a serving board for snacks. A tool roll such as those sold by Outdoor Research, containing spatulas and serving spoons, and containers for spices and cooking oil. A cellulose towel like the PakTowl, for drying dishes and picking up hot pots. A collapsible vinyl bucket for fetching water, and a collapsible wash basin for doing dishes.

An ideal cooking setup—dinner cooks on one stove while brownies bake in the Outback Oven.

I like plastic plates and bowls, but stainless steel works well, too. Lexan tableware is cheap and durable, but be careful around open flames—it will melt.

A useful accessory for warm-weather trips is a collapsible ice chest, which can keep such things as produce and butter fresh for several days. With two of these on group trips in the Sea of Cortez, I found that I could serve fresh foods for up to a week using wrapped dry ice as a cold source, even in daytime temperatures approaching 85 degrees F.

If you're paddling with a group of friends and are willing to share one kitchen among you, you can get really deluxe on cooking arrangements. For my guided tours, on which I had three single kayaks and two doubles among which to divide up the load, I developed a kitchen setup that eventually comprised a full-size, two-burner Coleman stove with a stand, a roll-up table, a large cutting board, full-size pots, an insulated coffee urn, a propane lantern and stand, several chef's knives, and even a cast-iron Dutch oven. It was a delight to prepare and cook food on standing-height surfaces with full-size implements, and to produce fresh peach cobbler from the Dutch oven for dessert.

Lighting

I live by a simple rule: You can never have too many flashlights. One experience of relying on a single flashlight for a major trip was lesson enough: The switch broke beyond repair and I was left to stumble about in the dark each evening.

My favorite all-around flashlight is the two-C-cell model made by Pelican Products, called the Super Peli-Lite (also sold by Browning). It has a simple twist switch that's nearly impossible to turn on accidentally and is immune to breakage. The C-cells provide a good compromise among bulk, brightness, and longevity, and the lights are completely waterproof. A Mini Maglite makes a good backup. I also carry spare bulbs for each light. Other good lights come from Princeton Tec.

Headlamps are a great way to provide hands-free lighting for many tasks. I like the kind that incorporate everything into the headband, instead of having a separate battery pack connected by a cord. Petzl makes several nice compact units.

Lamps and flashlights are fine for directed light, but for cooking, eating, and general camp lighting you want something more omnidirectional, like that provided by a lantern. Many models are available that use either white gas or LP canisters, and give a very bright and cheerful light. The only problem with these is the fragile wick, which can be destroyed by even moderate jostling; I usually take a half-dozen spares. An alternative is a battery-powered fluorescent lantern, the compact type that takes AA batteries; however, I've not had the best of luck with these—something always seems to be failing on them.

I absolutely have to read for a while before I can fall asleep at night, so I carry a battery-powered reading light, available at most bookstores. It saves battery life in my regular flashlights.

Okay—just one more. I carry a little light called a Surefire 6P by Laser Products. It takes two lithium cells, at about $5 each, and burns for only an hour. But you have to see the beam to believe it. Fire this thing up and sweep it around a campsite and it looks like a scene from *Stalag 17*. The lithium cells retain their energy for five years, so I keep the Surefire as an emergency light in case something really apocalyptic occurs, such as a kayak being blown offshore at night or a bear raiding camp. The only problem is restraint—it's so much fun to show this off when someone is demonstrating the power of his three-D-cell Mag-lite.

The candle lantern on the left is simple and reliable, but the gas lantern on the right puts out much more light.

Water Containers and Filter

If you don't need to carry a lot of water—say, under 2 gallons or so—then hard bottles such as Nalgenes work fine. However, when paddling in desert areas such as the Sea of Cortez you'll need a lot more than that for a long trip. I've loaded over 100 pounds of water in my kayak before any other gear went in for a weeklong

Baja trip in May. Ten or 12 gallons of water in ½-gallon Nalgenes is a real pain to pack—much better are flexible, 1- or 2-gallon containers, which can be squeezed between other gear.

I've used the inexpensive, transparent 2 ½-gallon "cubes" from Reliance, which only cost a few dollars; still, while they're tight and easily packed, they're also extremely prone to puncture by the smallest thorns or from abrasion inside the boat. Much better are the reinforced containers available from MSR and, if you can find them, Ortlieb. I came across a rep at a trade show jumping up and down on an Ortlieb water bladder filled with air, which satisfied me as to their toughness. For the budget minded, I'm told the Mylar bladders that hold wine-in-a-box are surprisingly tough when rinsed and used for water. To my mind, the only problem is that you first have to drink that wine.

Water purity should be of major concern to you when you're far from medical help. Although very few intestinal pathogens found in surface water in North America are likely to cause more than a couple of days of discomfort and some diarrhea, worse reactions are possible—and a severe case of dehydration from diarrhea and vomiting could be extremely dangerous without immediate access to a hospital. Recent research indicates that, at certain times of the year, up to 90 percent of the surface water in the United States is contaminated with some sort of intestinal pathogen. Idyllic visions of unspoiled wilderness notwithstanding, you should boil or filter any water you collect.

Boiling is simple and effective. You don't need to boil for any specific length of time; simply bringing the pot to a full boil will do the trick on any known pathogen. Boiling, however, is time consuming—especially if you need water in the middle of the day—and uses precious fuel. Iodine tablets are another time-honored fix, but they make for really lousy-tasting water. And pregnant women or anyone with thyroid problems should never use iodine products. Because of these hassles, more outdoor travelers are carrying some sort of mechanical device to treat their water.

Water-treatment units come in basically two types: filters and purifiers. *Filters* remove pathogens from the water by passing it through a very fine-pored material, either a membrane or a thick block. Filters can remove the relatively large organisms that cause about 99 percent of waterborne health problems: bacteria and protozoans.

Viruses, which are up to 1,000 times smaller than the above two groups, are nearly impossible to remove by means of filtering (although First Need has introduced a unit it says will filter viruses). Most *purifiers* use an iodine resin to kill viruses rather than remove them. Fortunately viral infection of surface water is vanishingly rare in first-world countries. Probably only if you were traveling to the nether regions of the world would you absolutely need a unit that removes or kills viruses.

My favorite water filter is one of the oldest: the Katadyn. It's difficult to pump compared to newer designs, and the output is slow, but the filter is absolutely reliable and, in contrast to products that need new filter cartridges every 200 gallons or so, the Katadyn will treat over *10,000* gallons—virtually a lifetime of normal use. Although the Katadyn is expensive to purchase, its long-term economy more than makes up for it. The Katadyn, however, will not kill or remove viruses. And I'm not as enamored of the newer, smaller Katadyn, which is a real pain to pump.

My second favorite filter is the Sweetwater, which costs around $50 and can be equipped with an optional iodine cartridge when and if you need it. The Sweetwater is compact and very easy to use, and the company will recycle old cartridges. The Sweetwater incorporates a charcoal element, which improves the taste of hard or chlorinated water.

If you use a water filter, take care not to contaminate the pure water with the incoming water. Don't wrap wet input and output hoses together when you store the unit (this is one reason the Katadyn has no output hose). Do not use any purifier that incorporates an iodine element if you are pregnant or suffer from a thyroid condition.

FOOD

There's rarely any reason to carry dehydrated or freeze-dried backpacking food on a kayaking trip. Most people run out of room in their boats before they run out of displacement (weight-carrying capability), so regular grocery items work just fine. Besides, the more closely you can approximate the diet you're used to at home, the less chance you'll have of any digestion problems while traveling.

If the climate permits, carry as much fresh food as possible, both for taste and the reasons mentioned above (er, unless you're *used* to a diet of prepackaged irradiated entrées). In the Pacific Northwest, for example, the cold water helps chill the inside of the boat, allowing fresh vegetables to keep for nearly as long as they would in your refrigerator at home. In Baja, on the other hand, you'll have to use a collapsible cooler and dry ice to maintain produce and dairy items.

Some foods store better than others. Cabbage keeps longer than lettuce, for example, and Roma tomatoes seem to hold up better than bigger varieties. New potatoes and baby carrots are tougher than their names suggest. And bagels stay fresh longer than loaf bread.

Although you should try to maintain the same *type* of diet you eat at home, your nutritional needs will be greater. You'll want breakfast foods high in complex carbohydrates, such as grain cereals or baked goods, and dried fruits. At night, especially if the weather is cold, you can eat foods higher in fat content—meats and cheeses—than might be good for you otherwise. Fats release a lot of energy, but they do so slowly and can leave you feeling sluggish if you eat fatty foods too early in the day. At night, on the other hand, fatty foods can help keep you warm while sleeping, and will recharge your metabolism for the next day. Much the same goes for proteins, which renew muscle and body tissue. And simple carbohydrates, such as the sugars found in sweet snack foods, are good for a quick energy boost but should not be relied on for long-term fuel.

For ease of cleanup, one-pot meals are the best. Casseroles, soups, stews, and the like can combine several food groups and provide a balanced meal. The ubiquitous Tuna Helper–type packages are good starting points; you can add vegetables and other ingredients to taste. Packaged noodle mixes such as Alfredo and ramen are other good starting points. And rice or pasta dishes are open for endless variation.

You can snack without guilt while kayaking; in fact, snacking is one of the best ways to keep your energy level high throughout the day. Granola bars, fruit leathers, or fresh or dried fruit are excellent, as are oatmeal cookies. Keep a few items in your deck bag or PFD pocket so you can munch without having to land.

PACKING THE KAYAK

It seems surprising, but a properly loaded kayak is much more stable than an empty one. A loaded boat has a lower center of gravity, so it's harder to capsize. The lower the boat sits in the water, the less area there is for the wind to push on and the longer the waterline becomes, increasing directional stability. But the load must be properly distributed to realize these gains.

Remember buying all those dry bags in different colors? Now is the time to take advantage of that, and organize your gear by color—breakfasts in the blue bag, clothes in the yellow one, and so forth.

Heavy items—water, canned food, and the like—should go as low in the boat as possible, and as close to both the centerline of the keel and the cockpit. I pack water right up against the rear bulkhead in the rear compartment, and against the front bulkhead in the front compartment. The lightest gear, such as your sleeping bag and tent, should be stuffed in the ends of the kayak. Make sure you keep the load balanced side to side, or the kayak will lean and try to turn in circles. Keeping weight out of the ends of the boat allows the bow and stern to ride up on waves instead of punching through them; it also makes turning much easier.

I try to put all my gear into dry bags, even things that don't really need protection from water. Bagged gear adds emergency flotation in the event of a leak or lost hatch (even fresh water adds a tiny bit of buoyancy, since it's lighter than salt water).

Once the gear is in place, ensure that it stays there. You don't want things shifting back and forth with every pitch of the boat. For me this is rarely a problem, since I take so much stuff there's little chance of anything moving. If the boat starts to get full, it's tempting to lash a dry bag or two on deck. Don't. Securing items on deck will destroy your low center of gravity and increase windage dramatically. Try to limit deck gear to one deck bag with snacks, camera, and the like inside.

SETTING UP CAMP

I make no excuses for being as comfortable as possible in camp. A comfortable camp is more restful, and a well-rested paddler is a stronger and safer paddler, one more alert to the beauty of the natural world—which is the whole reason for being out there.

The key to a comfortable camp is organization. If you take the time to pick a good site, properly arrange and set up your cooking, sleeping, and social areas, and strengthen the whole against wind and rain, you'll be free for the rest of your time there to relax and enjoy yourself. No chasing down windblown PFDs or food wrappers, no getting up at 2 A.M. to put on the tent fly or pound in extra stakes, no wondering where the toilet paper is.

Picking a campsite starts at the beginning of the day, when you examine the chart for the day's route. If you've not visited the area before look for likely camping spots on the chart, including small bays or inlets, islands, or protected headlands. Factor in what you know of local weather patterns such as wind and wave direction, precipitation, currents, and high and low temperatures to decide on likely spots. Use other factors as well. For example, in areas of high winds you might pick a cove with steep bluffs on the windward side for shelter; on the other hand, in an area of moderate winds but lots of biting insects, you might want to set up right out in the breeze to help keep the bugs down.

Tides are an important variable along some coasts. In certain parts of the Sea of Cortez, where the vertical tide range can exceed 20 feet, if you land on a flat beach at high tide and try to launch at low tide, you might have a $1/2$-mile portage to reach water. Use caution, too, in regions of fast tidal currents, especially around headlands that jut far out into the sea. You could land at slack water and find a dangerous current keeping you on shore later.

Planning is good, but don't lock yourself into one site first thing in the morning. If you chance upon a perfect spot 2 miles short of your goal for the day, for goodness' sake, stop.

Once you've located a site, the first thing to do is secure the kayaks above high-tide line. Read that again: The first thing to do is secure the kayaks above high-tide line. Don't just pull the boats above the last wet mark; find the highest storm-tide line you can and go beyond it to a point that, as near as you can determine, hasn't been submerged since the Pleistocene. Sea-kayaking literature is rife with tales of boats floated off on the tide and tents awash in brine.

With the boats momentarily safe, scout for a place to pitch the tent, if you're using one. The tent site forms the focal point of the camp. If at all possible, pick a flat spot or one you can flatten without permanently altering the landscape. If you cannot get a flat spot, orient the tent so your head will be uphill while sleeping; this is the least uncomfortable position in which to be tilted.

Don't place your campsite too close to a stream. Streamside vegetation tends to be fragile and easily destroyed by trampling. Also, you'll be more likely to attract mosquitoes and bears, both of which hang around water. And your toilet area should of course be far from any fresh water.

With a site selected, unload the kayaks, then immediately lock them down—put the spray skirt and PFD in one of the cargo compartments and resecure the hatch covers (alternatively, you can put the skirt and PFD in the cockpit and cover with a cockpit cover if you have one; if they need drying, stuff them under the deck bungees). Put the boats together side by side and lay your paddles between them; this keeps them from blowing away or getting stepped on in the dark. I like to tie the kayaks to something for extra security if possible; call me paranoid.

With the kayaks safe, pitch your tent. Always stake it down well, no matter how calm the weather has been. You should also put on the fly, even if no clouds threaten. The reason is that the coated fly is much less susceptible to ultraviolet deterioration than the uncoated canopy. Make sure the tent is taut, so it won't flap. Use as many guylines as necessary. If the ground is too soft to hold the stakes well, alternatives include piling rocks on top of the pounded-in stakes, tying a line to the middle of the stake and then wedging it behind two big rocks, or tying a line to a log or even one of the kayaks. Whatever you do, take the time to do it right so you don't have to worry when the wind comes up.

Even if I've stopped early I lay out my Therm-a-Rest pad inside now, with the valve open so it can inflate. I also lay out my sleeping bag so it can fluff. I carry a small dry bag with all the things I need at night: books, a reading light and regular flashlight, journal, and so forth. I toss this by the bed, and then put in my clothes bag and toilet kit. The bedroom is finished.

If I'm in bear country I set up the kitchen as far away from the tent as is practical, and downwind. I like to use local objects—rocks or logs—to elevate the stove and work surface above the ground if possible. It helps keep that gritty texture out of the food. I lay out the food bags somewhere in the shade, or suspend them in a tree if

These kayaks are well secured—far above the high-tide line, cockpit covers on and spray skirts inside, and paddles tucked between the boats.

bears might show up (at least 12 feet high). In the Arctic, of course, it would do you little good to suspend your food bags from a tree, given that a 50-year-old Arctic birch might be all of 4 inches tall. Just keep them well away from the tent—in fact, you shouldn't eat in your tent, or even store fragrant items such as sunscreen or toothpaste there in bear country.

A comfortable camp will greatly increase your enjoyment.

An option for treeless country is a bearproof food container, such as those manufactured by Garcia Machine. These cylindrical plastic containers don't allow the bear to get a grip with claws or teeth, and they do work, although they're decidedly awkward to store in a kayak. You could compromise with the smaller size, keeping just your opened and/or especially fragrant foods inside.

SANITATION AND LOW-IMPACT LAND USE

Schools of thought about the impact you should make on the natural world through which you travel range between two extremes. At one end is the old-fashioned approach: You carry an ax and cut down saplings for a new tent frame every night, construct comfortable latrines from split logs, dig ditches around your tent to channel off rainwater, and cook over a roaring fire with forked green branches holding your pots.

At the other extreme is the fanatical "no-impact" approach. This frowns on the use of toilet paper unless you carry it home with you, suggests drinking your leftover pasta-cooking water to avoid adding it to the environment, and would have building any type of campfire anytime be raised to a stoning offense.

While I try in every way possible to minimize my impact on the country through which I travel, I'm a bit uncomfortable with the idea that I should act as if I don't belong there, that any sign at all of my passage is some kind of sin. To me this forced separation of humans from the earth's doings is a fatal course, one that will lead to exactly the opposite of what its proponents wish. I know parents who genuinely care about the wild who won't let their children collect lizards or tadpoles to keep at home, who won't let them build tree forts or rock dams, whose every admonishment while in the wilderness is, "Look, don't touch." How will these children ever learn to appreciate the natural world if they're not allowed to interact with it? The answer is, they won't.

My philosophy is to use common sense to minimize the damage you create while traveling. In heavily traveled areas, use campsites already impacted so you don't disturb new ground; in virgin country, pick sites where you will have little impact yourself: gravel bars or sandy areas, bare spots of ground. Minimize fires, but if you want one, build it in a hollow on the beach. Avoid dumping lots of soap and detergent into the environment—use biodegradable products, and try scrubbing your pots with beach sand.

Shallow "cat holes" are better than deep holes for disposing of solid human waste, since the microorganisms that decompose such material stay near the surface. When possible, I carefully burn toilet paper.

CAMP PESTS

I've already talked a bit about bears, but the trouble you're most likely to face comes from a much smaller threat: insects. Mosquitoes and blackflies cause more misery than all the lions, tigers, and bears in the world.

In heavy insect country, a topical repellent is the most effective means of keeping them off you. Compounds incorporating DEET (N, N-diethyl-meta-toluamide) are extremely effective against mosquitoes, but beware any product containing more than 50 percent DEET—it's a highly toxic substance that can cause nervous-system damage. DEET is also ineffective against blackflies. Sawyer Products has a composite repellent called Sawyer Gold, with 16 percent DEET plus a compound known as R 326 to repel blackflies and gnats. I've tried it and it seems to work very well, although you'll need to apply it more often than a product with a higher DEET content.

Sadly, I've never had as much luck with natural repellents such as citronella, although citronella candles do seem to keep mosquitoes away. Another option in really bad situations is a head-net, which can be nearly 100 percent effective, if somewhat awkward. A product called Permethrin is available to apply to your tent door and other such areas (not on yourself) to help keep insects out of your living quarters.

If you're in bear country and want a means of self-defense, carry a can of capsicum spray with a content of at least 10 percent oleoresin capsicum, or one that advertises at least 2 million Scoville heat units (SHU). Buy a product designed to be used against bears; it will have a wider spray pattern than one intended for use against human attackers (although your bear spray will most certainly drop obnoxious humans in their tracks as well). These sprays have been proven effective in dozens of real-life encounters. One guide who inadvertently got between a mother grizzly and her cub—the worst of all possible bear scenarios—sprayed the momma when she charged to within 5 feet of him. The bear was so discomfitted by the burning pepper that she ran over her cub trying to get away. The best feature of pepper spray, of course, is that it results in no permanent harm to the animal.

When in bear country, make plenty of noise when hiking, and travel in groups if you can. If you are charged by a bear, *stand your ground*. Look at the ground, rather than into the bear's eyes. If all fails and you're attacked, with grizzlies the best defense is to play dead; however, recent research (did someone get a grant to go piss off bears?) indicates that you're better off fighting back—punching, kicking, yelling—if your attacker is a black bear. Just remember that the chances of actually being attacked are extremely low, especially if you take sensible precautions.

Many paddlers traveling in Baja and other desert areas worry about rattlesnakes and scorpions. There is one simple preventative measure: Watch where you put your hands, feet, and rear end. Scorpion stings—especially from the small, slender, members of the genus *Centruroides*—hurt like hell, but pose no danger to a healthy adult. A cold pack will help a bit. Scorpions hide under rocks, logs—and tents—during the day, and come out to hunt at night, so don't go barefoot if you have to answer the call at 2 A.M., and take care when you roll up your tent.

Rattlesnakes are very shy creatures whose only desire is to stay out of your way; even if you or someone you're with really screws up and is bitten, your chance of death is statistically very small. Carry an Extractor, a small vacuum pump made by Sawyer, which has been proven to remove a useful amount of venom if applied *immediately* after a bite. If you've got the space, do as I do and carry two Extractors, since the suction implement included with the tool will only fit over one fang wound at a time. Do not use a tourniquet, do not incise the bite, and do not immerse the bitten limb in ice. Also, don't administer codeine derivatives, which are vasodilators and can hasten the spread of venom. Get the victim to a hospital as soon as possible, where multiple doses of antivenin will be used to neutralize the venom. As I write this, research is nearing completion (although they've been saying that for about 10 years now) on a new type of antivenin that will be completely nonallergenic, and might be suitable for nonrefrigerated kits usable by laypeople.

I've had more mischief done by rodents than any other pest, and it's hard to get mad at them because they're so darn cute. One pocket mouse at a camp I frequented while guiding took to climbing in people's laps to steal food. A pack rat at another camp made off with a third of my Lexan tableware one night, apparently by leaping from an overhanging mesquite tree onto the kitchen table, jumping off with a fork or spoon in his teeth, then returning for another piece. Presumably he had already stolen someone else's plates and cups, and just needed the silverware to complete his set.

Many of my favorite moments sea kayaking have occurred while I wasn't even in the boat. I've covered 10 or 15—now and then 25 or 30—miles along a beautiful coast; near the end of the day I've found a sheltered cove and pitched a comfortable camp. After a hot supper I'll take the Therm-a-Lounger out to the beach and sit while the light fades from the sky and the stars appear one by one, then in groups, then constellations. Inland a pair of coyotes begin yapping; offshore a fin whale blows every few minutes. In these moments all is right with the world, so this is where I'll leave you. Happy and safe paddling.

APPENDIX 1

BUYING A USED KAYAK

Many newcomers to the sport of sea kayaking want their own boats but are understandably hesitant to sink $1,300 into a new plastic kayak, much less $2,000 or more into a new fiberglass model. Fortunately, used sea kayaks are easy to find in most seaport towns, and since the boats have so few moving parts, gambling on a previously owned example involves considerably fewer risks than buying a used car or computer. Nevertheless, careful inspection of the kayak is vital to ensure good service.

PLASTIC

Rotomolded sea kayaks are attractive to novices since they're both inexpensive and forgiving of the knocks and scrapes common to the learning process. But plastic kayaks do deteriorate over time and have a definite life span beyond which they should not be used, so shop carefully.

Polyethylene deteriorates in sunlight—more specifically, in ultraviolet light. With enough exposure the material becomes brittle and can split or even shatter with little warning, especially if it's roughly handled or dropped during freezing weather. This deterioration can happen in as little as a few years or can take 10 or more. Logically, a sea kayak used and left outside in Baja will have a much shorter service life than one paddled in the Pacific Northwest and stored in a garage (were I a pundit I might quip that a sea kayak in Seattle, where the chances of sun exposure are minimal, might be expected to last for centuries).

There are several ways to judge the condition of the plastic on a boat you're considering. First, look for the manufacturer's label in the cockpit. It will usually tell you when the boat was built; the date will either be listed by itself or encoded into the serial number—you can almost always decipher it. If the kayak was made more than five years or so previously, double the minuteness of your inspection.

A quick inspection of the deck lines and bungees will sometimes give you an idea of how much sun exposure the boat has had. I say *sometimes* because bungees and deck lines are easily replaced, so spiffy deck rigging is no guarantee of a sound hull. But if the lines are bleached and stiff, or frayed, you can be sure the kayak has seen its share of the outdoors.

Look for a chalky appearance on the plastic, particularly on the deck. Rub a finger briskly back and forth and see if a residue comes off; this will betray the beginnings of deterioration. Look under the deck lines to see if there are any "tan lines" where the plastic was protected from exposure. Of course, this residue is easy for a careful seller to remove with a bit of polishing; also, I've seen some badly degraded plastic hulls with no chalkiness at all.

Next, inspect the area around the through-deck fittings for tiny, spiderweb cracks. These are almost always a sign that the material is beginning to turn brittle. Still, don't reject the boat yet. Instead, look in the middle of large, unsupported areas of the hull and deck. If you see cracks there, leave quickly and find another boat—this one's ready to be converted to a planter. If there are only a few cracks around the fittings, and the kayak is less than five years old, it still might have some life left in it. However, you can use the cracks as a bargaining tool.

Once you're satisfied that the kayak hasn't reached senility, look carefully at the bottom of the hull for gouges that go more than halfway through. Gouges are difficult to repair on linear-polyethylene boats, and virtually impossible on cross-linked models. Also, check the hull for trueness—turn it over and sight down the keel line to make sure it's straight. If you can, check the way the boat has been stored to see if it's been supported properly (as well as kept out of the sun).

FIBERGLASS

As I mentioned in chapter 1, fiberglass is a nearly immortal material if it's not abused. So the age of a fiberglass kayak is nearly irrelevant, although the price will still be less on an older example.

The gelcoat provides the best means of determining how a fiberglass kayak has been cared for. If the deck is still glossy, it either has not had much exposure or has been waxed when needed. Unwaxed gelcoat will always develop a dull, chalky surface with prolonged use. If the seller has left dull gelcoat in place, ask whether you can try some automotive wax on a spot to see if it will polish out. Only the oldest or most badly treated gelcoat won't respond to waxing.

Obviously, you should look for cracks or splits in the fiberglass; however, even these can be fixed and are not in themselves reason to reject the boat. Deep gouges in the bottom gelcoat can be filled (this is much easier if the hull is white or off-white), as can serious scratches in the deck. Sometimes the manufacturer can match colored gelcoat for you, at least more closely than you could by messing around with mixing different hues yourself. Incidentally, minute cracks in the gelcoat around deck fittings are perfectly normal, so don't worry about them. Gelcoat is actually not very flexible, and this cracking in high-stress areas is unavoidable.

One place to inspect closely on a fiberglass kayak is the seam between hull and deck. There should be no evidence of looseness or leakage; if the boat looks as though it's been used hard, see if the owner will let you pour a few gallons of water inside, then tip the boat on both sides and back and forth to check for seam leaks.

I've seen a very few fiberglass kayaks with loose cockpit coamings. Check it, but remember that repairs are usually possible.

FOLDING KAYAKS

With care, folding kayaks can last decades. However, there are a lot more pieces to deal with than on a hard-shell boat, not to mention a fabric and Hypalon covering that must be treated properly to avoid problems.

Any prospective purchase of a folding kayak should include a complete assembly and disassembly. If the seller isn't willing to do this, I recommend walking away. With the boat in pieces, check the frame members for damage. In the case of a wood-framed boat, look carefully for signs of water intrusion in the wood, which can cause rot. The pieces should all have a good coat of varnish, and the alloy fittings on the ends should be tight. On aluminum frames, check that the pieces go together fairly easily (*every* aluminum-framed kayak I've ever used developed a few stubborn joints). On really tight joints, look for cracks, and check for corrosion around rivets. Fortunately, the pieces on folding kayaks can be replaced individually, so most problems can be corrected.

Abrasion is the enemy of the folding-kayak hull. Surprisingly, the outside bottom of the hull is often the least affected, since most manufacturers use thick Hypalon, which is incredibly tough. The place to check for abrasion damage is on the inside, where frame members rub against the hull material. If the owner hasn't been diligent in keeping sand out of the boat, it can cause significant problems. Ideally the hull has been stored unfolded, or at least only folded loosely, to minimize the risk of mildew and permanent creases.

OTHER FEATURES

Bulkheads

Bulkheads are frequently a source of trouble. Inspect them closely for looseness, and don't be surprised at what you find. Foam bulkheads on plastic boats are the most susceptible to loosening; fiberglass bulkheads on fiberglass kayaks virtually never come adrift. Bulkheads can be recaulked, but should be worth a reduction in price (unless it's already reflected). Stroking your chin and muttering, "Gee, those don't look very *safe*" is quite effective.

Rudders and Miscellany

As virtually the only moving part on the kayak, the rudder, while prone to little annoying failures, is easy to fix. The important thing is to confirm that the mounting points are solid, both for the foot pedals and for the blade assembly itself. Cables can be replaced—in fact, generally the whole bloody thing can be replaced if necessary (or a rudder added to a rudderless boat if you desire).

Inspect the seat-mounting bolts for tightness; if they're loose, check the holes to see if they have been worn too large by the bolt itself. Sometimes mounts can be redrilled in a slightly different spot with little problem, or the entire seat assembly replaced.

TEST DRIVE

If at all possible, arrange to paddle the kayak. This will reveal any significant problems such as leaks, or an out-of-true hull on a plastic boat (it won't track properly). A test paddle is essential if you've not already paddled an identical boat, to make sure it fits and works for you. Put the boat through as many paces as possible—turns, sprints, raising and lowering the rudder, and so on. Finally, try not to grin too widely as you paddle back toward the present owner, or your chances of bargaining will go right out the window.

APPENDIX 2

SOURCES

This list is not a complete catalog of all the excellent equipment and information resources available for kayakers. Any omissions are simply due to lack of space and are not intended as a comment on the quality of any gear or resources not listed.

BOAT MANUFACTURERS

Aire Inflatables
P.O. Box 3412
Boise, ID 83703
(208) 344-7506

Current Designs
U.S. office: Wenonah Canoe, Inc.
Box 247
Winona, MN 55987
(507) 454-5430

Dagger Kayaks
P.O. Box 1500
Harriman, TN 37748
(423) 882-0404

Easy Rider Kayaks
P.O. Box 88108
Seattle, WA 98138
(206) 228-3633

Eddyline Kayaks
1344 Ashten Road
Burlington, WA 98233
(360) 757-2300

Feathercraft Folding Kayaks
4-1244 Cartwright Street
Vancouver, BC V6H 3R8 Canada
(604) 681-8437

Kajak Sport
Mäntykankaantie 2
FIN-27100 Eurajoki
(358) 2-868-0844
(358) 2-868-0444 (fax)
kajaksport@utu.fi
www.utu.net/kajaksport/english.htm

Klepper Folding Kayaks
100 Cadillac Drive, Suite 117
Sacramento, CA 95825
(800) 323-3525

Mariner Kayaks
2134 Westlake Avenue North
Seattle, WA 98109
(206) 284-8404

Necky Kayaks
1100 Riverside Road
Abbotsford, BC V2S 7P1 Canada
(604) 850-1206

Northwest Kayaks
15145 NE 90th Street
Redmond, WA 98052
(206) 869-1107

Ocean Kayak (sit-on-tops)
2460 Salashan Loop
Ferndale, WA 98248
(800) 8-KAYAKS

P & H Designs
1107 Station Road, Unit 1
Bellport, NY 11713
(516) 286-1988

Pacific Water Sports
16055 Pacific Highway South
Seattle, WA 98188
(206) 246-9385

Perception
P.O. Box 8002
Easley, SC 29641
(803) 859-7518

Pygmy Boats (kits)
P.O. Box 1529
Port Townsend, WA 98368
(360) 385-6143

Rainforest Designs/Nimbus
6-9903 240 Street
Albion, BC V0M 1B0 Canada
(604) 467-9932

Southern Exposure Sea Kayaks
P.O. Box 4530
Location 18487 U.S. 1
Tequesta, FL 33469
(561) 575-4530

Valley Canoe Products/Great River Outfitters
4180 Elizabeth Lake Road
Waterford, MI 48328
(810) 683-4770
grokayak@ix.netcom.com

Wilderness Systems
1110 Surrett Drive
High Point, NC 27260
(910) 883-7410

PADDLING EQUIPMENT

PFDs

Extrasport
5305 NW 35th Court
Miami, FL 33142
(305) 633-2945

Lotus Designs
1060 Old Mars Mill Highway
Weaverville, NC 28787
(704) 689-2470

Palm Equipment/Great River Outfitters
4180 Elizabeth Lake Road
Waterford, MI 48328
(810) 683-4770

Seda
926 Coolidge Avenue
National City, CA 91950
(619) 336-2444

Stohlquist
P.O. Box 3059
Buena Vista, CA 81211
(719) 395-2422

Paddles

Aqua-Bound
1-9520 192nd Street
Surrey, BC V4N 3R8 Canada
(604) 882-2052

Cricket
17530 West Highway 50
Salida, CO 81201
(719) 539-5010

Eddyline/Swift Paddles
1344 Ashten Road
Burlington, WA 98233
(360) 757-2300

Lightning Paddles
22800 South Unger Road
Colton, OR 97017
(503) 824-2938
www.paddles.com

Nimbus Paddles
4915 Chisholm Street
Delta, BC V4K 2K6 Canada
(604) 940-1957

Sawyer Paddles
299 Rogue River Parkway
Talent, OR 97540
(541) 535-3606

Werner Paddles
P.O. Box 1139
Sultan, WA 98294
(800) 275-3311

Spray Skirts

Kokatat
5350 Ericson Way
Arcata, CA 95521
(800) 225-9749
(707) 822-7621

Palm/Rapidstyle Equipment
Great River Outfitters
4180 Elizabeth Lake Road
Waterford, MI 48328
(810) 683-4770

Perception
P.O. Box 8002
Easley, SC 29641
(803) 859-7518

Snap Dragon Design
14320 NE 21st Street, #15
Bellevue, WA 98007
(206) 957-3575

SAFETY EQUIPMENT

ACR Electronics (strobes, EPIRBS, lights)
5757 Ravenswood Road
Fort Lauderdale, FL 33312
(800) 432-0227

Adventure Medical Kits
P.O. Box 43309
Oakland, CA 94624
(800) 324-3517

Atwater Carey (medical kits)
1 Repel Road
Jackson, WI 53037
(414) 677-4121

Boulter of Earth (Driftstopper sea anchor)
46 Sussex Road
Washington Township, NJ 07675
(201) 722-0033

Gerber (multi-pliers, knives)
14200 SW 72nd Avenue
Portland, OR 97223
(503) 777-6905

Great River Outfitters (towing systems, deck pumps)
4180 Elizabeth Lake Road
Waterford, MI 48328
(810) 683-4770

Kayak Safe (spray-skirt release)
P.O. Box 1508
Mill Valley, CA 94941
(415) 381-1421

Motorola Sports Radios
1301 East Algonquin Road
Schaumberg, IL 60196
(800) 448-6686

Sea Wings (sponsons)
Georgian Bay Kayak
231 Gordon Drive
Penetanguishene, ON L9M 1Y2 Canada
(705) 549-3722
www.bconnex.net/~timkayak

See/Rescue (distress banners)
219 Koko Isle Circle, Suite 602
Honolulu, HI 96825
(800) 224-1123
seerescue@aol.com

Spyderco (knives)
4565 Highway 93
Golden, CO 80402
(303) 279-8383

West Marine (radios, Pains-Wessex flares, distress flags)
P.O. Box 50070
Watsonville, CA 95077
(800) 538-0775

CLOTHING, OUTERWEAR, AND FOOTWEAR

ExOfficio (clothing)
1419 Elliot Avenue West
Seattle, WA 98119
(800) 833-0831

Five-Ten (water shoes)
P.O. Box 1185
Redlands, CA 92373
(909) 798-4222

Kokatat (outerwear, dry suits)
5350 Ericson Way
Arcata, CA 95521
(800) 225-9749
(707) 822-7621

Patagonia (clothing, outerwear, water shoes)
259 West Santa Clara Street
Ventura, CA 93001
(805) 643-8616

RailRiders (clothing)
40 Smith Place
Cambridge, MA 02138
(617) 864-5969

Tarponwear (clothing)
P.O. Box 2272
Jackson, WY 83301
(307) 739-9755

Teva (sandals and water shoes)
1132 Mark Avenue
Carpinteria, CA 93013
(805) 684-1252

Vasque (water shoes)
314 Main Street
Red Wing, MN 55066
(612) 388-8211

ACCESSORIES FOR SEA KAYAKING

BDH (Safe Pack dry container)
available through Great River Outfitters
4180 Elizabeth Lake Road
Waterford, MI 48328
(810) 683-4770

Boulter of Earth (Driftstopper sea anchor, Sure-lock cable lock)
46 Sussex Road
Washington Township, NJ 07675
(201) 722-0033

Cascade Designs (dry bags, waterproof fanny packs)
4000 First Avenue South
Seattle, WA 98134
(206) 583-0583

Compac 50 (built-in bilge pump)
Henderson (Chimp bilge pump)
available through Great River Outfitters
4180 Elizabeth Lake Road
Waterford, MI 48328
(810) 683-4770

Dagger Canoe/Headwaters (accessories)
P.O. Box 1500
Harriman, TN 37748
(423) 882-0404

Kayak Safe (spray-skirt release)
P.O. Box 1508
Mill Valley, CA 94941
(415) 381-1421

Long Haul Products (Klepper, other folding kayak accessories)
2526 South Adams Street
Denver, CO 80210
(303) 782-9743

Mark Pack Works (deck bags, sails, paddle floats)
230 Madison Street
Oakland, CA 94607
(510) 452-0243

Oregon Scientific (electronic weather station)
available from Speedtech Instruments
10413 Deerfoot Drive
Great Falls, VA 22066
(800) 760-0004
www.speedtech.com

Ortlieb (map cases, dry bags)
available from NewSport
17650 140th Avenue SE
Renton, WA 98058
(800) 649-1763

Pelican Products (dry boxes, flashlights)
23215 Early Avenue
Torrance, CA 90505
(310) 326-4700

Primex (boat cart, sails, deck bags)
P.O. Box 505
Benicia, CA 94510
(800) 422-2482
primex@worldnet.att.net

Voyageur (dry bags, waterproof deck bags, accessories)
P.O. Box 610
Waitsfield, VT 05673
(802) 496-6247

RACKS AND TRAILERS

Bedrack (pickup rack)
Canyon Sports Racks
P.O. Box 502175
San Diego, CA 92150
(800) 414-9019

South Shore Kayaks (kayak saddles)
245 Main Street
Farmingdale, NY 11735
(516) 249-3537

Thule
42 Silvermine Road
Seymour, CT 06483
(203) 881-4832

Trailerlite (TerraPac trailer)
850A Calle Plano
Camarillo, CA 93012
(800) 854-8366

Yakima
P.O. Box 4899
Arcata, CA 95518
(800) 468-9000

CAMPING EQUIPMENT MANUFACTURERS

Adventure Foods
481 Banjo Lane
Whittier, NC 28789
(704) 497-7529

Basic Designs/Stearns (SunShower, accessories)
P.O. Box 1498
St. Cloud, MN 56302
(612) 252-1642

Bibler Tents/Black Diamond (single-wall tents)
2084 East 3900 South
Salt Lake City, UT 84124
(801) 278-5552

Black Diamond (expedition sewing kit)
2084 East 3900 South
Salt Lake City, UT 84124
(801) 278-5552

Camping Gaz/Bleuet (stoves, lanterns)
Suunto USA
2151 F Las Palmas Drive, Suite G
Carlsbad, CA 92009
(619) 931-9875

Cascade Designs (Therm-a-Rest, foam mattresses, Outback Oven, accessories)
4000 First Avenue South
Seattle, WA 98134
(206) 583-0583

Coleman (stoves, lanterns, sleeping bags, tents, accessories)
P.O. Box 2931
Wichita, KS 67201
(316) 832-2778

Crazy Creek (Therm-a-Lounger, camp chairs)
P.O. Box 1050
Red Lodge, MT 59068
(406) 446-3446

Garcia Machine (bearproof food containers)
14097 Avenue 272
Visalia, CA 93292
(209) 732-3785

Katadyn USA (water filters)
3019 North Scottsdale Avenue
Scottsdale, AZ 85251
(602) 990-3131

Laser Products (Sure-Fire Lights)
18300 Mount Baldy Circle
Fountain Valley, CA 92708
(800) 828-8809
www.surefire.com

Marmot Mountain International (tents, sleeping bags, clothing)
2321 Circadian Way
Santa Rosa, CA 95407
(707) 544-4590

Moss Tents (tents, Parawing)
P.O. Box 577
Camden, ME 04843
(207) 236-0505

Mountain Hardwear (tents, sleeping bags, outerwear)
950A Gilman Street
Berkeley, CA 94710
(510) 559-6700

MSR (stoves, cookware, water filters)
4225 Second Avenue South
Seattle, WA 98134
(206) 624-8573

The North Face
407 Merrill Avenue
Carbondale, CO 81623
(800) 719-6678
www.thenorthface.com

Outdoor Research (pouches, first aid, accessories)
2203 First Avenue South
Seattle, WA 98134
(206) 467-8197

Pelican Products (waterproof flashlights, boxes)
23215 Early Avenue
Torrance, CA 90505
(310) 326-4700

Petzl (headlamps)
PMI/Petzl Distribution
P.O. Box 803
Lafayette, GA 30728
(706) 764-1437

Primus (lanterns, stoves)
1462 U.S. Route 20
Cherry Valley, IL 61016
(815) 332-4951

Princeton Tec (waterproof flashlights, accessories)
P.O. Box 8057
Trenton, NJ 08650
(609) 298-9331

PÜR (water filters)
9300 North 75th Avenue
Minneapolis, MN 55428
(800) 845-7873

Sierra Designs (tents, bags, outerwear)
1255 Powell Street
Emeryville, CA 94608
(510) 450-9555

Sweetwater (water filters)
2505 Trade Center Avenue
Longmont, CO 80503
(303) 678-0447

BOATS, ACCESSORIES, AND RESOURCE RETAILERS BY MAIL AND INTERNET

Always patronize your local kayaking, outdoor, and bookstores first—it's good for your town's economy, good for making friends, and good for you, too (saves shipping and all the ancillary environmental costs associated therein). Use these resources if your local store cannot help you locate something.

Adventurous Traveler Bookstore
(800) 282-3963
books@atbook.com
www.AdventurousTraveler.com

Great River Outfitters
4180 Elizabeth Lake Road
Waterford, MI 48328
(810) 683-4770
grokayak@ix.netcom.com

Nantahala Outdoor Center
Outfitter's Store Mail Order
13077 Highway 19 West
Bryson City, NC 28713
(800) 367-3521
www.nocweb.com

Northwest Outdoor Center
2100 Westlake Avenue North
Seattle, WA 98109
(206) 281-9694

West Marine
P.O. Box 50070
Watsonville, CA 95077
(800) 538-0775

SCHOOLS FOR SEA-KAYAKING AND WILDERNESS SKILLS

This is only a partial listing of hundreds of good schools. Contact the Trade Association for Sea Kayaking or the North American Paddlesports Association for more resources.

Leave No Trace, Inc.
P.O. Box 997
Boulder, CO 80306
(303) 442-8222
(800) 332-4100

Monterey Bay Kayaks
693 Del Monte Avenue
Monterey, CA 93940
(408) 373-5397
www.montereykayaks.com

Nantahala Outdoor Center
13077 Highway 19 West
Bryson City, NC 28713
(888) 662-1662, ext. 600

National Outdoor Leadership School (NOLS)
288 Main Street
Lander, WY 82520
(800) 332-4100

Outward Bound
945 Pennsylvania Street
Denver, CO 80203
(307) 837-0880

Princeton University Outdoor Action Program
www.princeton.edu/~rcurtis/oa.html

Southwest Sea Kayaks
2590 Ingraham Street
San Diego, CA 92109
(619) 222-3616
kayaked@aol.com

Southwind Kayak Center
17855 Sky Park Circle #A
Irvine, CA 92714
(800) 768-8494

Wilderness Medical Associates
RFD 2 Box 890
Bryant Pond, ME 04219
(800) 742-2931

Wilderness Medicine Institute
P.O. Box 9
Pitkin, CO 81241

MAGAZINES

Atlantic Coastal Kayaker
P.O. Box 520
Ipswich, MA 01938

Canoe and Kayak
P.O. Box 7011
Red Oak, IA 51591
(712) 827-6363

Outside
400 Market Street
Santa Fe, NM 87501
(505) 989-7100
Annual buyer's guide, spring issue

Paddler
P.O. Box 697
Fallbrook, CA 92028
(619) 630-2293

Sea Kayaker magazine
7001 Seaview Avenue NW
Seattle, WA 98117
(206) 789-1326

Wave~Length
Gabriola Island, BC
(604) 247-9789
www.wavelengthmagazine.com

BOOKS

Paddling and Seamanship

Ashley Book of Knots. New York: Doubleday, 1993.

Burch, David. *Fundamentals of Kayak Navigation.* Old Saybrook, Conn.: The Globe Pequot Press, 1993.

Díaz, Ralph. *Complete Folding Kayaker.* Camden, Maine: Ragged Mountain Press, 1994.

Hanson, Jonathan. *Complete Sea Kayak Touring.* Camden, Maine: Ragged Mountain Press, 1998.

Hutchinson, Derek. *Eskimo Rolling.* 2nd ed. Camden, Maine: Ragged Mountain Press, 1994.

————. *The Complete Book of Sea Kayaking.* Old Saybrook, Conn.: The Globe Pequot Press, 1995.

Kellogg, Zip, ed. *The Whole Paddler's Catalog: Views, Reviews, and Resources.* Camden, Maine: Ragged Mountain Press, 1997.

Makower, Joel. *The Map Catalog: Every Kind of Map and Chart on the Earth and Even Some Above It.* New York: Tilden Press, 1992.

Seidman, David. *The Essential Sea Kayaker: A Complete Course for the Open Water Paddler.* Camden, Maine: Ragged Mountain Press, 1992.

Kayaking Adventure and Travel

Coffey, Maria. *A Boat in Our Baggage.* Camden, Maine: Ragged Mountain Press, 1995.

Lindemann, Hannes. *Alone at Sea.* Germany: Polner Verlag, 1992.

MacGregor, John. *A Thousand Miles in a Rob Roy Canoe.* London: British Canoe Union, 1963.

Nordby, Will, ed. *Seekers of the Horizon.* Old Saybrook, Conn.: The Globe Pequot Press, 1989.

Rogers, Joel W. *The Hidden Coast.* Bothell, Wash.: Alaska Northwest Books, 1991.

Taylor, Bill. *Commitments and Open Crossings.* London: Diadem Books, 1990.

Theroux, Paul. *The Happy Isles of Oceania.* New York: Ballantine Books, 1993.

General Outdoor

(With sections of interest to sea kayakers.)

Getchell, Annie. *The Essential Outdoor Gear Manual: Equipment Care & Repair for Outdoorspeople.* Camden, Maine: Ragged Mountain Press, 1995.

Hampton, Bruce, and David Cole. *Soft Paths: How to Enjoy the Wilderness Without Harming It.* Mechanicsburg, Penn.: Stackpole Books, 1995.

Hanson, Jonathan, and Roseann Beggy Hanson. *Ragged Mountain Press Guide to Outdoor Sports.* Camden, Maine: Ragged Mountain Press, 1997.

Ilg, Steve. *The Outdoor Athlete: Total Training for Outdoor Performance.* Evergreen, Colo.: Cordillera Press, 1989.

McMenamin, Paul, et al. *The Ultimate Adventure Sourcebook: The Complete Resource for Adventure Sports and Travel.* Atlanta: Turner Publishing, 1992.

Meyer, Kathleen. *How to Shit in the Woods: An Environmentally Sound Approach to a Lost Art.* Berkeley, Calif.: Ten Speed Press, 1989.

Petzoldt, Paul. *The New Wilderness Handbook.* New York: W. W. Norton, 1984.

Waterman, Laura, and Guy Waterman. *Backwoods Ethics: Environmental Issues for Hikers and Campers.* Woodstock, Vt.: Countryman Press, 1993.

————. *Wilderness Ethics: Preserving the Spirit of Wildness.* Woodstock, Vt.: Countryman Press, 1993.

First Aid and Sports Medicine

Auerbach, Paul S., M.D. *Medicine for the Outdoors: A Guide to Emergency Medical Procedures and First Aid.* Revised and expanded ed. New York: The Lyons Press, 1999.

Breyfogle, Newell. *Commonsense Outdoor Medicine and Emergency Companion.* 3rd ed. Camden, Maine: Ragged Mountain Press, 1994.

Forgey, William W., M.D. *Hypothermia: Death by Exposure.* Merrillville, Ind.: ICS Books, 1985.

Gill, Paul Jr., M.D. *The Onboard Medical Handbook: First Aid and Emergency Medicine Afloat.* Camden, Maine: International Marine, 1997.

Southmayd, William, M.D., and Marshall Hoffman. *Sports Health: The Complete Book of Athletic Injuries.* New York: Perigee Books, 1984.

Cooking

Daniel, Linda. *Kayak Cookery*. Old Saybrook, Conn.: The Globe Pequot Press, 1988.

Jacobson, Don. *The One Pan Gourmet: Fresh Food on the Trail*. Camden, Maine: Ragged Mountain Press, 1993.

Kesselheim, Alan S. *The Lightweight Gourmet: Drying and Cooking Food for the Outdoor Life*. Camden, Maine: Ragged Mountain Press, 1995.

Miller, Dorcas. *Good Food for Camp and Trail: All-Natural Recipes for Delicious Meals Outdoors*. Boulder, Colo.: Pruett Publishing Company, 1993.

Spangenberg, Jean and Samuel. *The Portable Baker: Baking on Boat and Trail*. Camden, Maine: Ragged Mountain Press, 1997.

VIDEOS

Performance Sea Kayaking: The Basics . . . and Beyond (Performance Video and Instruction, Inc., Durango, Colo.; 970-259-1361).

WEATHER

NOAA (National Oceanic and Atmospheric Administration), Network Information Center Weather Page, www.nnic.noaa.gov

Reifsnyder, William E. *Weathering the Wilderness: The Sierra Club Guide to Practical Meteorology*. San Francisco: Sierra Club Books, 1980.

EVENTS AND SYMPOSIA

Cape Breton Seakayak Symposium, sponsored by Island Seafari Seakayaking, Louisbourg, Nova Scotia; (902) 733-2309 (July).

Trade Association of Sea Kayaking (TASK), Mequon, WI; (414) 242-5228; sponsors the following symposia:

- East Coast Canoe and Kayak Symposium (April)
- Chesapeake PaddleFest (May)
- Alaska Sea Kayak Symposium (May)
- West Coast Sea Kayak Symposium (September)

ORGANIZATIONS

Sea Kayaking

Trade Association of Sea Kayaking
12455 North Wauwatosa Road
Mequon, WI 53097
(414) 242-5228
www.halcyon.com/wtr/TASK.html

North American Paddlesports Association
12455 North Wauwatosa Road
Mequon, WI 53097
(414) 242-5228
www.halcyon.com/wtr/watersports_resources.html.

Conservation

(Organizations that have ocean-related conservation campaigns.)

Cousteau Society
Chesapeake, VA
(804) 523-9335
www.sky.net/~emily/cousteau.soc/

National Audubon Society
700 Broadway
New York, NY 10003
(212) 979-3000

Sea Shepherd Conservation Society
P.O. Box 628
Venice, CA 90294
(310) 301-7325
www.seashepherd.org

Sierra Club
85 Second Street, 2nd Floor
San Francisco, CA 94105
(415) 977-5500

ON THE WEB

Please be aware that World Wide Web page addresses (URLs, or Uniform Resource Locators) change frequently. If you cannot find a page listed below, try searching for the subject in a global search engine, such as Lycos, Infoseek, or Magellan.

GORP (Great Outdoor Recreation Pages), www.gorp.com/

General Paddling Information News Group (includes whitewater), news:rec.paddle

Outside Online, outside.starwave.com

Yahoo Outdoor Pages, www.yahoo.com/entertainment/outdoors

Yahoo Outdoor Magazines Reference Page, www.yahoo.com/ entertainment/outdoors/magazines/

GEAR AND PROVISIONING LISTS

MASTER LIST

Paddling Gear

Boat	Paddles	Spray skirt
PFD	Bilge pump	Bailer
Sponge	Security cable	Cockpit cover
Compass	Deck bag	Dry bags and boxes

Safety Equipment

Meteor flares	Parachute flares	Paddle float
Signal mirror	Whistle	Strobe
VHF radio	Sea anchor	Smoke flares
Handheld flares	EPIRB	See/Rescue banner
Tow line	Sea Wings	Barometer
Knife	Anemometer	

Navigation

Charts	Compass	Tide tables
Dividers	Map measurer	Straightedge
GPS	Pilot guide	Pencil
Chart case		

Kitchen

Fuel bottle(s)	Pot scrubber	Cooking knife
Stove	Dish soap	Spatula
Stove repair kit	Cooking oil	Spices
Heat diffuser	Pots	Pot gripper
Frying pan	Griddle	Outback Oven
Utensils	Matches	Large spoon
Whisk	Bowls	Measuring cup
Plates	Paper towels	Cups
Trash bags	Grater	Aluminum foil
Can opener	Containers	Bottle opener
Ziploc bags	Coffee filters	Grill
Filter holder	Spice kit	Thermos
Egg holder		Water bottles
Water filter		

Bedroom

Tent	Ground cloth	Stakes
Tarp	Parawing	Therm-a-Rest
Therm-a-Lounger	Sleeping bag	Bag liner
Pillow	Guylines	Awning poles

Bathroom

Soap/Sea soap	Shampoo	Towel
Toothbrush	Toothpaste	Mirror
Comb	Brush	Deodorant
Razor	Lotion	SunShower
Toilet paper	Matches	Trowel

Medical Kit

Sunscreen	Insect repellent	Hydrocortisone cream
Band-Aids	Chap Stick	Dressings
SAM splint	Bandage shears	Sting-eze swabs
Thermometer	Sawyer Extractor	Hemostats
Forceps	Moleskin	Spenco 2nd Skin
Ace bandage	Elbow support	Needle
Eye pads	Adhesive tape	Cold packs
Knuckle bandages	Irrigation syringe	Butterfly closures
Antiseptic swabs	Dental kit	10% iodine solution
Dramamine	Aspirin	Acetaminophen
Antihistamine	Ibuprofen	Pepto-Bismol tablets
Mylanta	Imodium	Aloe vera gel
Prescription drugs	EpiPen	Eyedrops

Clothing

Pants	Shirts	Underwear
Hats	Socks	Fleece jacket
Paddling jacket	Wet suit	Dry suit
Thermal stretch suit	Gloves	Booties
Hiking shoes	Water shoes	Sandals
Thermal underwear	Shorts	Sweater
Bandannas	Pogies	Rubber boots
Belt	Sunglasses	

Miscellaneous

Flashlight	Spare flashlight	Batteries
Spare bulbs	Lantern	Spare mantles
Fanny pack	Binoculars	Camera equipment
Fishing gear	Field guides	Naturalist's gear
Journal	Snorkeling gear	Bear repellent

ABOUT THE AUTHOR

Author and naturalist Jonathan Hanson has been a kayaking pro since the 1980s. He has operated his own kayak touring company, guiding clients to many locations in the Sea of Cortes, both on the mainland and Baja coasts. His own trips have taken him from Mexico to the Arctic Ocean and many places in between. His many articles on sea kayaking have appeared in *Outside, Sea Kayaker, National Geographic Explorer,* and other publications. He has also written six books, including *Complete Sea Kayak Touring* (Ragged Mountain Press, 1998), and has a sea kayak destination book forthcoming from W.W. Norton. A biologist by training, Jonathan lives in the Chiricahua Mountains in southeastern Arizona with his wife, Roseann, with whom he has co-authored numerous natural history and outdoor books.

INDEX